Waikīkī

Nine Walks Through Time

EXPLORING HISTORIC AND CONTEMPORARY SITES IN WAIKĪKĪ

Bird's eye view of Waikīkī

by
Veneeta Acson, Ph.D.

ISLAND HERITAGE

Photographs © 2003 Michi Atkinson

ALL RIGHTS RESERVED

Copyright ©2003 Island Heritage Publishing
No portion of this book may be reproduced, in whole or in part, in any form or by any means, electronic or mechanical, including photocopying, recording, or by any information storage and retrieval system now known or hereafter invented, without prior written permission from Island Heritage Publishing.

Printed in China

ISBN: 0-89610-479-6

Produced, published, and distributed by:

94-411 Kō'aki Street, Waipahu, Hawai'i 96797
For Orders: (800) 468-2800 For Information: (808) 564-8800
Fax: (808) 564-8877
islandheritage.com

Serves 9

FUDGE IN A BAG

In a gallon-size zippered freezer bag, combine 4 oz. softened cream cheese, 2 T. softened butter, 3 C. powdered sugar, and ½ C. unsweetened cocoa powder. Seal the bag and knead with your hands to mix everything together. Be patient – keep mashing and squeezing until all the dry ingredients are worked in and a ball of fudge forms. Flatten the ball into a square while it's still in the bag. Cut the bag open and remove the fudge slab to a cutting board. Slice into pieces with a pizza cutter and decorate with M&Ms if you'd like. Easiest fudge ever!

Makes 24

PINWHEEL COOKIES

You'll Need

- ¾ C. butter, softened
- 1½ C. sugar
- 2 eggs
- 1½ tsp. vanilla
- 3 C. all-purpose flour
- 1 tsp. baking powder
- ½ tsp. salt
- Food coloring
- 24 cookie sticks
- Glaze *(recipe on page 63)*
- Decorating sugar or sprinkles, optional

DEDICATION

*In memory of my mother, Alice Acson,
who loved living in Waikīkī.*

*To my children, Nicholas and Samantha,
who have learned to love Waikīkī.*

*To my husband and best friend, Howard Z.
Streicher, who loves all things Hawaiian.*

Waikīkī Beach at dusk (Veronica Carmona)

FOREWORD

THE FIRST EDITION OF THIS BOOK APPEARED IN 1983. I am proud to say that it was among the first books to describe the real Waikīkī, not just the glittery hotels and restaurants. Since then, several other books about Waikīkī, especially some beautiful "coffee table" books, have been published. Much has happened in those intervening years, not only in Waikīkī, but also in the United States and our world.

The major changes in Waikīkī occurred with the disappearance of some old, charming buildings, such as the former *Fong's Inn* at 2051 Kalākaua Avenue and *Buckminster Fuller's Geodesic Dome*, which has been replaced by the newest Hilton hotel building, Kālia Tower of the Hilton Hawaiian Village.

On the other hand, a site that the 1983 book predicted would be demolished is still now standing in all its glory: Waikīkī Theater (**Walk IV**).

Other sites are still standing, but much improved and better integrated into the Hawaiian life: the Kāhuna Stones (**Walk IX**) and 'Āinahau Park/Princess Ka'iulani Park (**Walk V**).

This book is intended for Waikīkī visitors, *kama'āina*, and tourism employees:
• Tourists curious about their fabled vacation spot,
• Residents proud of their special home, and
• Tourism employees hoping to acquire and share a greater knowledge and understanding of their unique working place.

Every attempt has been made to make this book factual and accurate. Places and events that eluded satisfactory verification have been noted, as for instance, the historic layout of Puaaliilii[+] (**Walk III**) and the location of *Kalehuawehe* (**Walks III** and **VIII**).

For the most part, controversies over sites, place names, and spelling have not been emphasized. These controversies certainly do exist. I hope this book will stir up greater pride and interest in Waikīkī. Waikīkī today needs all the *aloha* it deserves.

[+]Read **Walk III** for a discussion of the two spellings and interpretations of this place name, depending on the placement of the Hawaiian markings.

Early Waikīkī beach with Diamond Head in the background. (Hawaiʻi State Archives)

CONTENTS

Foreword   **v**

An Introduction to Waikīkī   **viii**

Hawaiian Place Names   **x**

Notes about the Walks   **x**

Hawaiian Language and Guide to Pronunciation   **xii**

Hawaiian Spelling   **xiii**

The Hawaiian Monarchy and Important Dates
   since the End of the Monarchy   **xiv**

Hawaiian Glossary   **xv**

Acknowledgements   **xvii**

Overall Map   **xviii**

Walk I: Ala Wai Canal   **1**

Walk II: Early Hawaiian Life in Waikīkī: *Kālia*   **15**
             Hawaiian Taro Fields and Fishponds
             Chinese Rice Fields and Duck Ponds

Walk III: Early Royalty   **31**

Walk IV: Miracle Mile: Waikīkī from the 1930s
               through the 1950s   **39**

Walk V: Last Days of the Monarchy   **53**

Walk VI: Local Life Today in Waikīkī   **67**

Walk VII: Kapiʻolani Park and Honolulu Zoo   **77**

Walk VIII: Foot of Diamond Head   **87**

Walk IX: Beach Walk   **99**

Further Reading   **118**

Index   **119**

AN INTRODUCTION TO WAIKĪKĪ

Waikīkī means 'spouting, shooting, or spurting water' (*wai* means 'water,' as in the Ala Wai Canal, or the 'water way'). Waikīkī's name refers to the great abundance of freshwater in the area. Before the 1920s, several streams

Men torch-fishing (Hawai'i State Archives)

flowed from the mountains, across the valley floors, across Waikīkī, and into the Pacific Ocean. Three large streams, *Pi'inaio*, *'Āpuakēhau*, and *Kuekaunahi*, provided Waikīkī with an effective natural irrigation system. For the early Hawaiians, this led to an intricate aquaculture system of taro fields and fishponds. When the Chinese arrived in the nineteenth century, they added rice fields and duck ponds. However, in the 1920s these streams were all filled in with the material that was dredged from the Ala Wai Canal. Fortunately, the location where each stream emptied into the Pacific Ocean is known: *Pi'inaio Stream*, near the 'Ilikai Hotel; *'Āpuakēhau Stream*, at the Outrigger Hotel; and *Kuekaunahi Stream*, 'Ewa of Kapahulu Pier.

Waikīkī is located on the island of O'ahu, 157°50' W and 21°17' N, approximately 1,500 miles (2,400 kilometers) from the equator. This location has blessed Waikīkī with enviable weather: an all-time low of 49 degrees in December 1999, and an all-time high of 95 degrees in October 1984, September 1986, and again in July 1987. However, the average high is 84 and the low, 70. An average annual rainfall of 20 inches keeps the vegetation green. A perfect climate!

The physical boundaries of modern-day Waikīkī are defined with reference to the Ala Wai Canal, the Pacific Ocean, and Diamond Head. However, the boundaries of historic Waikīkī were far broader. Waikīkī was an *ahupua'a*, which is a large, pie-shaped land division extending from the mountain crest to the ocean. Although it is difficult to reconcile historical records and maps with present-day locations, it appears that the Waikīkī *ahupua'a* extended to Ward Avenue in the west and to the Kuli'ou'ou Ridge in Hawai'i Kai in the east. In the Mahele of 1848, the land division, the lands of Hawai'i were chopped up, divided, appropriated, and distributed, resulting in today's smaller land units. Kamehameha III enacted land reform, moving from the traditional Hawaiian system of crown-owned land to a system of private ownership, thus paving the way for subsequent development.

When Mā'ilikūkahi became king in the fourteenth century, he was taken by the chiefs to reside in Waikīkī. That event may mark the origin of the long tradition of royal residences there.

One of the earliest available accounts of Waikīkī was written in 1792 by the English explorer Captain George Vancouver. He described the numerous and large villages along the shores of Waikīkī ("Whyteete," as he wrote it) with vast, wet taro fields and an abundance of waterfowl (**Walk II**).

Waikīkī's first hotel, Hotel Waikīkī, opened in 1837. Several hotels opened in the 1880s and 1890s: *Sans Souci* in 1884; *Park Beach* in 1888; and *Waikīkī Seaside* in 1894 (**Walks VIII** and **IX**). In 1901, the time was ripe for a large deluxe hotel in the very center of the beach area: the Moana Hotel. The Moana was so successful that in 1918, its owners built an addition.

Ala Wai Canal and buildings today

A drastic change in the topography and development of Waikīkī occurred with the building of the Ala Wai Drainage Canal, as it was called at its inception. The excavation of the canal and the diversion of Waikīkī's streams resulted in the intentional drying up of the ponds and fields. Coral dredged from the canal bed was used to fill in the dried-up areas. The building of hotels and, more recently, condominiums followed.

As the Ala Wai Canal was being completed in the late 1920s, another large hotel was also being completed: the Royal Hawaiian Hotel (**Walk IX**). This hotel was opened in 1927 with the expectation that tourism would

Royal Hawaiian Hotel

continue to grow. Unfortunately, the stock market crash two years later and the depression that followed reduced tourism to a low point during those years. Business remained minimal during World War II as Waikīkī was virtually closed down: the Royal Hawaiian Hotel housed navy personnel, barbed wire went up along Kalākaua Avenue, the Natatorium was used for training soldiers, and President Roosevelt held conferences at the *Deering-Holmes Estate* (**Walks VIII** and **IX**).

Over the years, Waikīkī's beach sand has been altered by erosion and by the construction of buildings close to the shore. During the past eighty years, there have been changes in the composition of the sand along the beaches. Thousands of tons of sand have been imported from places on O'ahu (mainly Kāne'ohe Bay), neighbor islands (Moloka'i and Maui), and reportedly from as far away as California.

Today it is estimated that twenty thousand people live in Waikīkī and more than thirty-five thousand people work in Waikīkī. On an average day, there are sixty-five thousand visitors to Waikīkī!

Welcome to Waikīkī!

HAWAIIAN PLACE NAMES

The Hawaiians named every significant patch of earth and water to emphasize the importance of these places. Today, many traditional place names survive only as names of streets.

Most streets in Hawai'i have Hawaiian names. In *Place Names of Hawai'i,* by Pukui, Elbert, and Mookini, it is estimated that 86 percent of the place names in this state are of Hawaiian origin. In Waikīkī, approximately two-thirds of the street names are Hawaiian. The other third are mostly English surnames of Waikīkī residents and landowners.

Waikīkī street sign (I-31)

Although a large proportion of island residents today are of Asian ancestry, there are few Asian place names on O'ahu. This is partly due, on the one hand, to the tradition of naming streets for Hawaiian royalty, aspects of Hawaiian culture, and landowners, and on the other hand, to a Honolulu city ordinance that requires all new and renamed streets to have Hawaiian names. Most Asians came to Hawai'i as individual laborers. Only in later years did they establish families and permanent homes. There are only a few Chinese-based and Japanese-based place names and no Filipino place names at all, due to late immigration arrival dates.

Many events in Hawaiian history are widely known today only as street names. At least, in this way, those names provide a basis of familiarity for learning about Hawai'i's past. Furthermore, an awareness of their significance makes being here more fun!

NOTES ABOUT THE WALKS

You may use this book as a guide for walking tours or simply read it to learn more about historic and contemporary Waikīkī. If you read it straight through, you may note that some facts and anecdotes are repeated. Since certain facts, people, and events occur in several walks, some information is repeated in each walk so that you can stick to one section and not flip back and forth.

The walks are indicated with Roman numerals, the stops or sites with Arabic numerals.

The accompanying photographs illustrate places of the past in brownish tones or in wavy frames and interesting present-day locations in color.

Contemporary sites appear in regular type; historic sites in italics.

The titles for each walk attempt to evoke the essence of each area covered. Below each title are the layers of history that you can encounter in Waikīkī. These seven discrete layers include:
• Present–day structure
• Post–World War II
• Post–Ala Wai Canal: 1920s to World War II
• Pre–Ala Wai Canal: 1880s to 1920s
• Late monarchies to annexation

- Early monarchies up to Kamehameha I
- Legends

Most stops do not have more than two or three layers of history, but who knows—for the next edition of this book, historians may have uncovered even more. We are always on the lookout for new information.

Walks I and **IX** are linear—that is, they are straight-line walks from one end of Waikīkī to the other. The two walks combine and encircle Waikīkī. **Walk I** follows the canal; **Walk IX** goes along the beach.

Walks II through **VIII** focus on smaller areas encircled by **Walks I** and **IX**. These central walks meander among the streets of Waikīkī.

The order in which you take the walks may vary, depending on your time and inclination. The times vary from half an hour (**Walk III**) to two hours (**Walk VIII**), with most walks lasting one and one-half hours. The recommended time of day for the walks is early morning before the heat of the noonday sun, especially in summer.

Always wear protective clothing, sunglasses, a hat, comfortable shoes, and sunscreen.

The emphasis of the tours ranges from historical to modern neighborhood and lifestyles.

For example, a history buff might enjoy the following chronological order:
  III Early Royalty
  V Last Days of the Monarchy
  I Ala Wai Canal
  IV Miracle Mile (Waikīkī, 1930s through 1950s)

If you are interested in modern lifestyles and the development of Waikīkī, you might consider the following sequence:
  IV Miracle Mile
  VI Local Life Today in Waikīkī

Most people who live in Hawai'i use a particularly local way to indicate directions. Rather than the traditional compass directions of north, south, east, and west, the people of Hawai'i use local landmarks and place names:
- *makai*: toward the sea
- *mauka*: toward the mountains
- Diamond Head: in the direction of Diamond Head (in an easterly direction)
- 'Ewa: in the direction of the plantation town of 'Ewa (in a westerly direction) [in this word, the w is pronounced like a v]

These direction designations will be used throughout the book—look for the compass rose on each map (Diamond Head and *'Ewa* are terms used only in Honolulu [including Waikīkī]. In other parts of the island and on other islands, other terms replace them.)

Due to the changing tide and shifting sands of progress, the walker is cautioned that some of the sites may suddenly disappear.

Happy walking!

HAWAIIAN LANGUAGE AND GUIDE TO PRONUNCIATION

Hawaiian belongs to the Polynesian language family—a group of about thirty languages, most of which lie within a triangle formed with Hawai'i, Rapa Nui (Easter Island), and Ao Te Roa (New Zealand) at the corners. Polynesian is, in turn, part of a larger language family, Austronesian, which includes many more related languages in Melanesia, Micronesia, the Philippines, Indonesia, Malaysia, and even as far away as Taiwan and Madagascar.

The Reverend Hiram Bingham and his wife, Sybil Moseley Bingham. Bingham played a major role in creating a written form for the Hawaiian language. (Hawai'i State Archives)

Although many explorers and traders wrote Hawaiian words according to how they heard them, it was Protestant missionaries who first studied the language systematically in the 1820s and developed an alphabet, modified only slightly since that time. Once you know how this efficient writing system works, you can spell any word you hear, and pronounce any word you read.

The short vowels are pronounced as follows:

a as in *ah* (but shorter in duration). The a changes to an *uh* sound before the vowels *i* or *u*, even if it's in the next syllable.
e as in *bait* (without the glide after the vowel)
i as in *beat* (without the glide after the vowel)
o as in *boat* (without the glide after the vowel)
u as in *boot* (without the glide after the vowel)

A long vowel (e.g., ā, ē, ī, ō, ū), marked with a line over it called a *kahakō*, or macron, is similar to a short vowel in quality, but is simply longer. This difference is important: for example, *kau* means 'to put,' but *kāu* means 'your.' Certain vowels combine to form diphthongs: *ai, au, ae, ao, ei, eu, oi, ou*, and *iu*. In a diphthong, the first vowel is always accented, no matter where it appears in a word.

The consonants are pronounced as follows:

h, l, m, and **n** as in English.
p and **k** as in English, but without the puff of air you can hear in words like *pay* and *key*.
w varies between an English *v* and *w*, tending toward *w* after the vowels *u* and *o*.
' (*'okina*—glottal stop) is similar to the sound in the middle of *uh-oh*. Like any other consonant, it can change the meaning of a word. For example, *kou* means 'your'; *ko'u* means 'my.'

Every syllable contains a vowel or diphthong, and it may or may not be preceded by a consonant. For example, a-lo-ha shows both kinds of syllables. As the example shows, no syllable (or word) can end with a consonant.

Accent is predictable only in short words: it falls on the second-to-last syllable, on a long vowel, or on a diphthong. Longer words can be divided into accent units, each of which behaves like a short word. In the word lists in this book, accent units in longer words are separated by a period. This is a system used in Pukui and Elbert's *Hawaiian Dictionary*. Thus, *aka.mai* 'smart' is pronounced *áka.mái*, with slightly more emphasis on the last unit. (This marking is not part of the official spelling, but is only a way to show you where the accents are.)

As you become more familiar with some common Hawaiian words, you'll begin to recognize them when they appear in longer words. For example, *Uluniu* 'coconut grove' is made up of two common words: *ulu* 'grove' and *niu* 'coconut.' The pronunciation reflects this as well: the word is accented *úlu.níu.* This example also shows that adjectives follow nouns (grove-coconut)—just the opposite of English.

The glossary and the index contain Hawaiian words used in this work. To show the accent in longer words, periods separate accent units, as in the examples given.

HAWAIIAN SPELLING

The first Hawaiian alphabet, dating to the 1820s, has been slightly modified. This is because the missionaries did not hear all the distinctive sounds of the language. In particular, they were unable to hear the glottal stop and long vowels. However, the previous examples show how important these distinctions are. Writing Hawaiian without them is like writing English without several of the consonants and half the vowels. Still, in most cases, native speakers (and readers) were able to use context to decide which word was actually meant in a spelling such as *pau* (which could be any of these words: *pau* 'finished,' *pa'ū* 'moist,' *pa'u* 'soot,' or *pā'ū* 'sarong').

On the other hand, words out of context are a problem. Since Hawaiian was written for well over a century without marking the glottal stop and long vowels, the proper pronunciation of some uncommon words has been lost. Therefore, you might see some variation in the spelling of words. For example, Kahekili, chief of Maui, is often spelled with a macron over the first vowel: Kāhekili. Another example is Kuekaunahi Stream. Both the meaning and the correct pronunciation have been lost. Therefore, the correct spelling is uncertain. To reflect this discrepancy, an asterisk (*) has been placed before words like this in the index.

Another wrinkle in the system comes from the Bible, which was translated into Hawaiian long before the glottal stop and macron were part of the alphabet. Because of its sacredness, many present-day Christian Hawaiians believe that since their Bible did not use these markings, Hawaiian words today should not use them either.

THE HAWAIIAN MONARCHY AND IMPORTANT DATES SINCE THE END OF THE MONARCHY

Ruler	Also Known As	Lived	Ruled
Kamehameha I	Kamehameha the Great	1748/61–1819	1810–1819
Kamehameha II	Liholiho	1797–1824	1819–1824
Kamehameha III	Kauikeaouli	1814–1854	1825–1854
Kamehameha IV	Alexander Liholiho	1834–1863	1854–1863
Kamehameha V	Lot Kamehameha	1830–1872	1863–1872
Lunalilo+	William C. Lunalilo	1835–1874	1873–1874
Kalākaua++	David Kalākaua King David The Merrie Monarch	1836–1891	1874–1891
Lili'uokalani	Queen Lydia	1838–1917	1891–1893

+First monarch to be appointed by the Hawaiian legislature
++First monarch to be elected by the Hawaiian legislature

OTHER ROYALTY:

Queen Ka'ahumanu	King Kamehameha I's favorite wife
Queen Keopuolani	King Kamehameha I's sacred wife
Queen Emma	King Kamehameha IV's wife
Queen Kapi'olani	wife of King Kalākaua
Princess Likelike	sister of Kalākaua and Lili'uokalani
Princess Ka'iulani	daughter of Governor Cleghorn and Princess Likelike

Kamehameha I (1758–1819) in a 1819 Louis Choris portrait (Hawai'i State Archives)

IMPORTANT DATES SINCE THE MONARCHY:

Provisional government	January 17, 1893
Republic of Hawai'i	July 4, 1894
U.S. Annexation	August 12, 1898
U.S. Territory of Hawai'i	July 14, 1900
Statehood	August 21, 1959

HAWAIIAN GLOSSARY

Hawaiian words are in *italics*, followed by English translations. For more detailed translations, see the *Hawaiian Dictionary*, by Pukui and Elbert.

ahi fire
'ahi yellow-fin tuna
ahu.pua'a a large, historic land division that extended roughly from the mountain crest to the ocean, often marked by a pile of stones (*ahu*) with an image of a pig (*pua'a*) on top
'ai to eat
'āina land
aka.mai smart
'ā.kia kind of shrub
ala way, path
ali'i chief, royalty
aloha love, pity, affection
'alohi to shine; bright
'ape large taro-like plant, "elephant ears"
'ā.pua fish trap; handle
'au.'au to bathe

'Ewa the direction away from Diamond Head, toward the plantation town of 'Ewa (past Pearl Harbor); in a westerly direction

hale house
hali'a remembrance
hamo.hamo to pat
hau native hibiscus; dew
hei.au religious structure
helu to scratch; to count
hua fruit
hula native dance with chanting

i to (object marker)
ihe spear
'ili land section; surface
'ili.'ili pebble
'ilima native shrub
'io hawk
'iu heights

ka the
kaha to soar
kahi place
kahikai seaside
kahuna a professional specialist in religion, education, or medicine; later used especially for a Hawaiian priest/sorcerer. The plural is *kāhuna*.
kai sea, seawater
kalo a plant that is the main staple of the Hawaiian diet; all parts are edible: the leaves are used as *lū'au* and the starchy root as *poi*
kama.'āina literally 'child of the land': a person born and reared in the islands; sometimes extended to include people who have lived in Hawai'i for a very long time but were born elsewhere

"Iles Sandwich: Femme d'Isle Maui Dansant." *A Maui dancer performs a* hula kuhi lima *(seated dance without instruments). (Hawai'i State Archives)*

kanaka person, human
kāne male
kaona hidden meaning
kapa bark cloth
kapu taboo
kau to put
kāu your
kaua battle
kau.kahi singleness of purpose
ke the
kea white
kē.hau dew
kī ti plant
kiawe algaroba (mesquite)
kī.kī spouting, shooting
kio protuberance
koa *Acacia koa* tree
kou your; a native tree
ko'u my
kua back
kua.hiwi mountain
kue fishhook
kū.lia to strive

lā day
la'a sacred
lae forehead
lama type of wood like ebony
lā.nai veranda
lani heaven, royal height; very high chief, high-born one
lau leaf
lau.a'e type of fern
lehua flower of the *'ōhi'a* tree
lei garland
lei pā.pale hat *lei*
lei po'o head *lei*
li'i.li'i little
limu seaweed
lī.poa type of seaweed
loa long, tall
lo'i irrigated terrace, especially of taro
loko pond, lake

lua pit
lua.kini temple, *heiau*
lū.'au feast

mahele division
Mahele the division of the land under Kamehameha III in 1848. This was a time when all the land of the islands was divided up and either given to chiefs or commoners, or kept for the crown.
mahuka to flee, escape
mā.kā.hā lock, sluice
makai (*ma kai*) toward the sea
mā.kā.lei fish trap
makani wind
malu.hia peace; safety

1874 Kanaka Maoli *(native full-blooded Hawaiian)* *(Hawai'i State Archives)*

mā.noa vast
maoli native
mauka (*ma uka*) toward inland
mea thing
moa chicken
moana ocean
mō.'ī chief
moku island
mo'o lizard

nā (plural)
naio seaweed; false sandalwood
nani beautiful
nau.paka mountain or seashore shrub

nau.paka kaha.kai seaside *naupaka*
nau.paka kua.hiwi mountain *naupaka*
niu coconut
nui big
nu'u height

'ohana family
'ō.hi'a two kinds of tree—mountain apple and *lehua*
'ō.hua retainer, servant
'okina glottal stop
'oli.'oli joy
'ō.paka.paka blue snapper

pā.lolo clay
paoa strong odor
pā.pale hat
pau finished
pa'u soot
pa'ū moist
pā.'ū sarong
pe'e to hide
pi'i to go inland, climb
pī.kake peacock; jasmine
pi'o arch
poi taro paste, Hawaiian staple
poni coronation
poni.mō.'ī carnation

po'o head
pua flower, child
pua'a pig
puka perforation, hole
pu'u hill

'ula red
ulu grove
'ulu breadfruit
'ulu maika a bowling-like game; stones for the game

wai freshwater; liquid of any kind other than seawater
walina softness
wehe.wehe opening in reef

Pikake and maile lei (IH image library)

ACKNOWLEDGEMENTS

Many thanks to Dale Madden and Roxane Kozuma at Island Heritage who had the foresight to reedit this book.

Thanks to Albert J. Schütz for encouraging me to revise the book, twenty years later, and for editing the sections on the Hawaiian language, guide to pronunciation, and Hawaiian spelling.

Many thanks to my Honolulu hosts, Robert and Bernice Littman, for their unending philoxenia and love.

Thanks to my walking buddy and fellow linguist, Kent Sakoda.

Mahalo to the Waikīkī Historic Trail *'ohana* for picking up the gauntlet and educating us about the years gone by. I loved walking with you! *Mahalo nui loa* especially to Cha, Joe, and Kamealoha. Continue your excellent work!

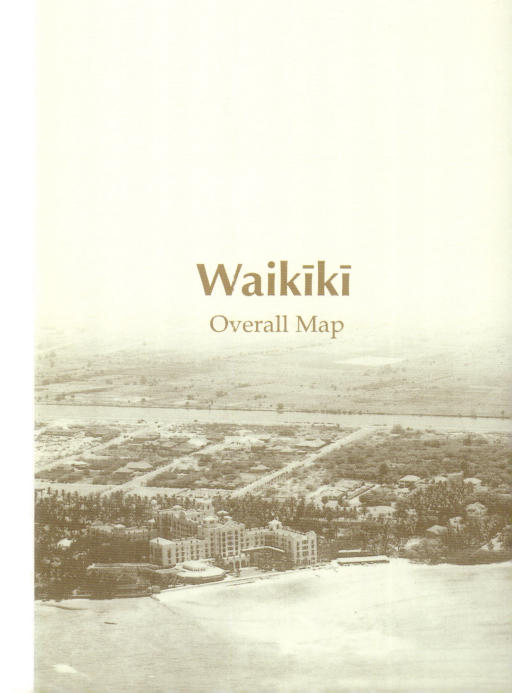

Waikīkī
Overall Map

THIS IS AN OVERALL MAP OF WAIKĪKĪ, INDICATING THE NINE WALKS.

> **Maps:**
>
> Detailed maps accompany each walk and show the stops along the route.

Some of these individual maps are overlaid in blue-green to indicate the waters that once crossed the area.

The overlays are based on several maps dating from 1891 to 1897.

Until the construction of the Ala Wai Canal in the 1920s, Waikīkī had three main streams and many fishponds, duck ponds, rice fields, and taro fields.

Waikīkī Beach and Beyond, ca. 1930 (Hawai'i State Archives)

Walk I
· Ala Wai Canal ·

Walk I
Ala Wai Canal
The entire length of the canal

🕐 **TIME:** 1.5 hours
➪ **DISTANCE:** 2 miles (3 kilometers)

Ala Wai Canal

THE DREDGING OF THE ALA WAI CANAL WAS PROPOSED AS EARLY AS 1905, BUT ACTUAL WORK BEGAN IN 1921. The project was dubbed the Waikīkī Reclamation Project. By 1928 the Waikīkī Drainage Canal, as it was originally called, was completed, thereby drastically altering not only the topography, lifestyle, and fate of the area known today as Waikīkī, but also the life of the Hawaiian people.

The original topography of the area included three streams running from the mountains into the valleys and through Waikīkī, each emptying directly into the Pacific Ocean. Waikolu Way, a small street crossing Lewers Street near Kūhiō Avenue, is reminiscent of those three streams: *Waikolu* means 'three waters.'

Those three rivers, beginning from the Diamond Head side and overlaid in blue-green on the accompanying map, are *Kuekaunahi Stream*, *'Āpuakēhau Stream*, and *Pi'inaio Stream*.
- *Kuekaunahi Stream* met the ocean near Kūhiō Beach Park.
- *'Āpuakēhau Stream* had its outlet near present-day Outrigger Hotel.
- *Pi'inaio Stream* exited 'Ewa of Duke Kahanamoku Beach and Lagoon.

All three of those former stream outlets are visited in **Walks II, III**, and **IX**.

The three streams furnished Waikīkī with a natural irrigation system. The entire area from the Ala Moana Shopping Center to Kapi'olani Park was replete with taro fields, fishponds, and migrant ducks. After the arrival of the Chinese in the nineteenth century, rice fields and ponds for domesticated ducks were added.

By 1900, O'ahu businessmen recognized the fantastic development potential of the Waikīkī area. The beaches had long been famous for their beauty and charm, but the neighboring ponds and fields came to be seen as obstacles to Waikīkī's development. Soon, financial interests dictated that these fields and ponds be eliminated. Vast quantities of coral removed in the canal's dredging were used as fill, thus raising Waikīkī to its average current elevation of six feet above sea level.

Along with the disappearance of the taro and rice fields and fish and duck ponds, a way of life for the Hawaiian people vanished. ♣

WALK I ❖ ALA WAI CANAL

Ala Wai Canal

> ➤ **BEGIN WALK:** *This walk starts on the* mauka *'mountain' side of Ala Wai Boulevard at 'Āinakea Way, one block 'Ewa of Kapahulu Avenue. (It can also begin at the other end, stop **I-32** or **I-33**, reviewing the stops in reverse order.)*
>
> *There are many benches along the way, so you can stop, rest, and read in the shade as you go along. Also notice the bi-level Victorian lampposts. And, as the signs warn, do not eat the fish!*

1. Ala Wai Canal / Ala Wai Golf Course and Club

Ala Wai means 'fresh waterway,' referring to the streams that empty into it from the mountains and valleys. Originally the canal was to empty into the Pacific Ocean at both ends. By the late 1920s, however, when the canal had reached its present configuration, funds for the project were exhausted.

The Ala Wai Canal is approximately 2 miles (3.2 kilometers) long and, originally, varied in depth from 10 to 20 feet (3 to 6.5 meters). Today, due to lack of dredging, the deepest point is only 5 meters. The canal serves a watershed area of approximately 16 square miles. The Ala Wai Canal is not lined with a cement floor, unlike most other drainage canals and streams in Hawai'i. It is carved out of natural solid coral.

The Ala Wai Golf Course, a 146-acre municipal course located on the *mauka* side of the canal, extends to the Mānoa-Pālolo Drainage Canal (**I-17**) on the 'Ewa side. The golf course is laced with remnants of earlier streams.

 It is said to be the busiest golf course in the United States, and perhaps one of the most active in the world, reportedly with almost two hundred thousand rounds of golf played here in one year.

The original nine-hole golf course opened on September 13, 1931, as the first municipal course in Hawai'i. It was built on the site of the Territorial Fairgrounds on 150 acres of land. The second nine holes were opened on July 10, 1937, with one of the structures at the fair serving as its clubhouse. In 1948, a new clubhouse was built, named after Francis 'Ī'ī Brown, "the father of golf in Hawai'i." In 1989, a $5.8 million clubhouse was constructed. The first labor force to maintain the links came from the Territorial O'ahu Prison.

Local lore says that the origin of the golf course dates to the early 1920s, when two local men sank a can where hole number six is now located for their on-the-spot golf course! However, another story recounts that Territorial Fairgrounds caretakers set up their own course, charging twenty-five cents a hole!

As you walk along the canal you will see small bridges, drainage holes, and drainage canals on the *mauka* side. Some of the streams still follow their earlier courses as shown in blue-green on the accompanying map, but many have been diverted or altered. Both sides of the canal are lined with date and coconut palm trees. On the Diamond Head end of the canal are a few *hau* trees, formerly abundant in Waikīkī. *Hau* belongs to the Malvaeceae (mallow) family, which

❖ 4 ❖

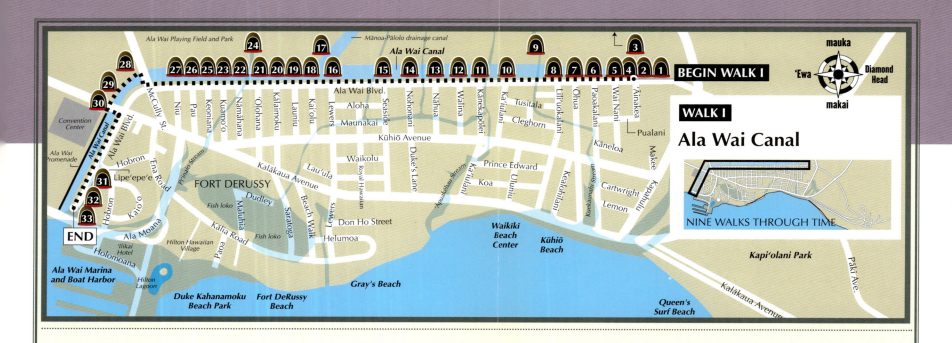

Walk I
Ala Wai Canal

- I-1 Ala Wai Canal Ala Wai Golf Course and Club
- I-2 'Āinakea Way
- I-3 Ridges, Valleys, and Neighborhoods Beyond Waikīkī
- I-4 *Kuekaunahi Stream*
- I-5 Wai Nani Way
- I-6 Paoakalani Street
- I-7 'Ōhua Avenue
- I-8 Lili'uokalani Avenue
- I-9 *'Āpuakēhau Stream*
- I-10 Ka'iulani Avenue
- I-11 Kānekapōlei Street
- I-12 Walina Street
- I-13 Nāhua Street
- I-14 Nohonani Street
- I-15 Seaside Avenue
- I-16 Lewers Street
- I-17 Mānoa-Pālolo Drainage Canal
- I-18 Kai'olu Street
- I-19 Launiu Street
- I-20 Kālaimoku Street
- I-21 'Olohana Street
- I-22 Nāmāhana Street
- I-23 Kuamo'o Street
- I-24 *Pi'inaio Stream*
- I-25 Keoniana Street
- I-26 Pa'ū Street
- I-27 Niu Street
- I-28 McCully Street
- I-29 Makiki Stream
- I-30 Kalākaua Avenue
- I-31 Līpe'epe'e Street
- I-32 Ala Wai Promenade
- I-33 McDuff Park

Waikīkī Coconut Grove, ca. 1890 (Hawai'i State Archives)

ALA WAI CANAL ✤ **WALK I**

Waikīkī—Ala Wai Canal (Hawai'i State Archives)

includes the hibiscus. In the course of its life (one day!), the *hau* blossom displays three different colors: yellow upon opening, then bright orange, and finally red-brown when it drops. The *hau* tree had many traditional uses: its rough but lightweight wood was used for making canoe outriggers; its fibers were made into rope; and its sap and flowers were used medicinally. There are still many areas of *hau* along the beach today. Just look for a hibiscus-like flower.

On the *mauka* side of the Ala Wai Canal are several groups of outrigger canoes waiting to be lowered into the canal. In the afternoons, after work and school, men, women, and children come to the canal to practice their strokes. Be sure to come in the afternoon to watch them—it's very picturesque!

The view of the downtown skyscrapers downstream from the Diamond Head end is very impressive.

Continue walking along the *makai* 'toward the sea' side of the canal. Each street name you encounter will be described and its name translated.

Some street names appear arbitrarily; others are interrelated with neighboring streets, such as Paoakalani (**I-6**), meaning 'royal perfume,' and the three streets following it. These four streets relate to Queen Lili'uokalani.

Enjoy the scenery of Waikīkī's lovely and underutilized open space as you walk. It was once proposed that the convention center be built here. It was ultimately built *'Ewa* of here, near the Ala Moana Shopping Center, at Kalākaua Avenue and Kapi'olani Boulevard.

 'Āinakea Way

'Āinakea means 'white land.' Its name refers to the appearance of a type of sugarcane grown in the islands.

 Ridges, Valleys, and Neighborhoods Beyond Waikīkī

Sit on a bench along the canal while you relax and read.

The canal is an excellent vantage point for viewing the ridges and

WALK 1 ⁒ ALA WAI CANAL

Ridges beyond Waikīkī

valleys of the Koʻolau Mountains that provide an imposing backdrop for Waikīkī and are the location of several of Honolulu's main residential districts. Off to the right, across the canal, is the district of Kaimukī, a neighborhood of one- and two-story homes situated on the ʻEwa side of Diamond Head. *Kaimukī* means 'the ti (*kī* in Hawaiian) oven' or 'oven for cooking the ti root.' Ti is an indigenous (local) plant of the lily family and its leaves have been used for roofing, food wrapping, *hula* skirts, and sandals. The ti root was cooked and used for food and distilling liquor. Today the many varieties of the ti plant are widely used in ornamental plantings around the islands. Its leaf is

Ti plant

still used in present-day Hawaiian cooking—for example, it is wrapped around butterfish for cooking, and the fish is served in its wrapper. Be sure to try real Hawaiian food before you leave the islands!

The valley directly ahead is Pālolo Valley, a neighborhood of small homes. Its name refers to a type of clay. Above Pālolo Valley on the right is Wilhelmina Rise, named for one of the Matson Navigation Company ships. Matson built the Princess Kaʻiulani Hotel and the Royal Hawaiian Hotel, and also took over the ownership of the Moana Hotel. In 1959 Matson sold these hotels to the Japanese company Kyo-Ya, which owns them to this day. To the left of Pālolo Valley is St. Louis Heights, named for a school located on its slopes.

Below St. Louis Heights on the left lies Mānoa Valley, the largest valley on this side of Oʻahu. *Mānoa* means 'vast.' The main campus of the University of Hawaiʻi is located in this cool, lush valley. On a hot day, it's a treat to hike toward the end of the valley to Mānoa Falls.

Between Mānoa Valley and the Ala Wai Canal is Mōʻiliʻili, a residential and commercial district. *Mōʻiliʻili* means 'pebble lizard.' According to Hawaiian legend, this name refers to a lizard destroyed by Hiʻiaka, sister of the volcano goddess, Pele.

The smaller valley to the left is Makiki Valley. Makiki is a type of octopus lure made of heavy stone. This densely populated residential area is the site of numerous condominium buildings.

This site—and anywhere along the canal—offers an excellent viewing point for late-afternoon double rainbows. Double rainbows, which are often seen in Hawai'i after a light rainfall, consist of a bright main rainbow below a fainter outside rainbow. The outside rainbow is always a mirror image of the main rainbow, and its colors are in reverse order. Perhaps you have noticed the two rainbows on the side of the Hilton Hawaiian Village's Rainbow Tower: this is not a true double rainbow because it is not in mirror image (**II-14**).

Ala Wai and valleys

 Kuekaunahi Stream

The water emptying into the canal across the way may be a remnant of *Kuekaunahi Stream*, which once flowed into Waikīkī at this approximate area. The fresh waters (recall **I-1**, Ala Wai) flowed down from the mountains above Pālolo Valley, through this section, and emptied into the Pacific Ocean, Diamond Head of Kūhiō Beach Park (**IX-16 to 18**).

With the construction of the Ala Wai Canal, *Kuekaunahi Stream* was forever lost to history as it was diverted into the canal further upstream. The meaning and even the correct Hawaiian spelling of *Kuekaunahi* have grown obscure with the passage of time; however, *kue* means 'fishhook.'

Queen Lili'uokalani
(Hawai'i State Archives)

The next four streets, which abut Ala Wai Boulevard, recall the reign of Hawai'i's last ruling monarch, Queen Lili'uokalani. The queen lived from 1838 to 1917 but ruled slightly less than two years, from 1891 to 1893.

Queen Lili'uokalani owned a large tract of land in this part of Waikīkī, extending from the Ala Wai Canal to the beach between Lili'uokalani Avenue and Wai Nani Way, connecting with a 1,400-foot strip of beachfront land. This area was known as *Hamohamo*, meaning 'rub gently,' referring perhaps to the action of the water on the sand. The queen owned two homes in Waikīkī: one in this area, the other closer to the beach.

 Wai Nani Way

Wai Nani means 'beautiful water' and most likely refers to the beautiful *Kuekaunahi Stream*, which flowed though the queen's land.

WALK I ❖ ALA WAI CANAL

 Paoakalani Street

Paoakalani means the 'royal perfume.' This was the name of one of Queen Lili'uokalani's homes, which was located between Paoakalani and Wai Nani on the other side of Ala Wai Boulevard. (None of those streets was in existence at the time, of course.)

Notice the abundant hibiscus bushes along the canal.

 'Ōhua Avenue

'Ōhua means 'retainer' or 'servant' and refers to the retainers of King Kalākaua and of Queen Lili'uokalani, who were housed along this street.

The building across the canal is the clubhouse of the Ala Wai Golf Course.

 Lili'uokalani Avenue

This street obviously commemorates Queen Lili'uokalani, whose name literally means 'smarting of the highborn one.' This queen was so named, local lore tells us, because on the day of her birth, her foster mother's aunt was suffering from eye pain.

She wrote the story of her life in *Hawaii's Story by Hawaii's Queen*. This fascinating account of her life and the lives of those around her is illustrated and includes genealogies and appendices of major documents and events during her lifetime. The author is simply, Lili'uokalani.

 'Āpuakēhau Stream

The small, bridged, palm-lined stream across the canal may be one of the courses of historic *'Āpuakēhau Stream* as it entered Waikīkī. *'Āpuakēhau* means 'basket of dew.'

The stream's name may refer to the vast quantities of *hau* and palm trees and ti plants that lined its banks. *'Āpuakēhau*, the middle of Waikīkī's three streams, flowed from the mountains above Mānoa Valley, passed through the *'Āinahau* property where Princess Ka'iulani lived (**V-1**), and emptied into the ocean *'Ewa* of the Moana Hotel. *'Āpuakēhau* was the best known of Waikīkī's waterways because it flowed beside the royal residence and also gave its name to the nearby *heiau*, a Hawaiian 'open-air religious structure' (**III-4**).

Notice the outrigger canoes along the *mauka* bank.

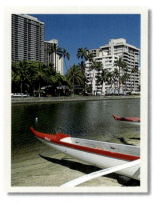

Ala Wai Canal

 Ka'iulani Avenue

Ka'iulani means 'the sacred height' and is named in honor of Princess Ka'iulani, who lived *makai* of here with her parents. The family called this area *'Āinahau* (**V-1**).

Kānekapōlei Street

This is the half-mile point from the Diamond Head end of the canal.

Kānekapōlei is the name of a god of flowers. This street was named for Marion Kānekapōlei Guerrero Diamond, a resident of this area in the 1930s, who was named for an uncle of a wife of King Kamehameha I.

 ### Walina Street

Walina means 'softness.'

The bridged stream across the canal may have been a branch of ʻĀpuakēhau Stream.

 ### Nāhua Street

Nāhua means 'the fruits.' This street is named for Nāhua, a Hawaiian chiefess who owned land between the Royal Hawaiian and Halekūlani hotels.

 ### Nohonani Street

Nohonani means 'sit daintily.' This is a poetic phrase often used in songs honoring royalty, Liliʻuokalani in particular.

 ### Seaside Avenue

This street is named for the *Waikīkī Seaside Hotel*, which preceded the Royal Hawaiian Hotel from 1894 to 1927 (**IX-9**).

 ### Lewers Street

Originally called Lewers Road, this is the longest north/south street in Waikīkī proper. At the turn of the nineteenth century, two Lewers families lived in Hawaiʻi. The street is most likely named for the Robert Lewers family, who resided at the present site of the Halekūlani Hotel (**IX-5**) at the other end of Lewers Street.

Mānoa-Pālolo Drainage Canal

 ### Mānoa-Pālolo Drainage Canal

This canal is so named because it drains water from both the Mānoa and Pālolo streams, each flowing out from its respective valley (**I-3**) and joining together just *mauka* of the H-1 Freeway. The diversion and displacement of these streams came about with the installation of the Ala Wai Canal in the 1920s.

ʻ*Ewa* of the Mānoa-Pālolo Drainage Canal is the Ala Wai Playing Field and Park.

 ### Kaiʻolu Street

Kaiʻolu means 'cool ocean.'

 ### Launiu Street

Launiu means 'coconut leaf.'

This is the one-mile mark from the Diamond Head end of the Ala Wai Canal.

The next five streets are named for people associated with the first two Kamehamehas:
- King Kamehameha I (Kamehameha the Great), who lived from the mid 18th century to 1819, and united the islands in 1810.
- King Kamehameha II (Liholiho), who lived from 1797 to 1824, but reigned only during his last five years.

 Kālaimoku Street

Kālaimoku means 'island manager' or 'island carver.' This street was named for a prime minister under King Kamehameha I and Queen Kaʻahumanu. Kālaimoku died in 1827.

Looking directly across the canal from Kālaimoku Street is University Avenue, which leads into Mānoa Valley and the University of Hawaiʻi at Mānoa.

 ʻOlohana Street

ʻOlohana was the Hawaiian name of John Young I, a castaway English sailor who was stranded in 1790 at Kealakekua, Hawaiʻi (the Big Island), where Captain Cook was killed. ʻOlohana became the principal advisor to Kamehameha I and helped the king invade and conquer Maui. ʻOlohana married Kuamoʻo (**I-23**), a niece of Kamehameha I. One of his grandchildren

Kamehameha II (1797–1824) (Hawaiʻi State Archives)

was Queen Emma, wife of Kamehameha IV. ʻOlohana died in 1835.

The name ʻOlohana is said to be a transliterated Hawaiian borrowing of the English phrase "All hands!" which Young reportedly shouted at his fellow sailors. Interestingly, the verb *ʻolohani* means 'to strike' or 'to mutiny.'

 Nāmāhana Street

Nāmāhana means 'twins' or 'double' and is also the Hawaiian name for the constellation known in English as the Twins, Castor and Pollux, *Nānā Mua* and *Nānā Hope*, respectively.

Nāmāhana is also the name of daughters of Keʻeaumoku of Maui and Kamehameha I, as well as the name of a Maui chiefess.

 Kuamoʻo Street

Kuamoʻo means 'back of the lizard.' This street was named for a niece of Kamehameha I, who was the second wife of ʻOlohana (**I-21**).

Kuamoʻo, in turn, had been named in honor of the place where her brother was killed in an 1820 battle fought over the breaking of an eating *kapu* (taboo). At that time, women were forbidden to eat with men and were allowed to eat only certain foods. For example, only two types of bananas were permitted to be eaten by women; all other varieties were *kapu*. (Incidentally, the free-to-choose-who-to-eat-with-and-what-to-eat side won!)

 Piʻinaio Stream

Today this is known as Makiki Stream. The exact meaning of *Piʻinaio* has been lost, although *pi'i* means 'to climb' or 'to go inland,' and *naio* can refer either to a type of seaweed or to the false sandalwood that grows in Hawai'i.

 Keoniana Street

Keoniana is a transliterated Hawaiian borrowing of the English name John Young. The street is named for John Young II, son of 'Olohana (**I-21**), who served as *kahuna nui*, or executive officer, under Kamehameha II and as minister of foreign affairs under Kamehameha IV.

The author's mother, who inspired the writing of this book, lived at 439 Keoniana in the 1970s.

 Pa'ū Street

Pa'ū, meaning 'moist' or 'damp,' is named for the surrounding area and a nearby pond that was part of the Hawaiian agricultural and aquacultural system. The pond was first used for fish and taro growing, and later, when the Chinese moved into the area, ducks and rice were introduced (**Walk II**).

Pa'ū Street today is a heavily traveled route connecting Ala Moana Boulevard with McCully Street (**I-28**).

This word, *pa'ū*, shows the importance of marking long vowels and glottal stops in the Hawaiian spelling system:

> *pau*, with no diacritics, means 'finished.'
> *pa'u*, with a glottal stop between the *a* and the *u*, means 'soot' or 'tedious labor.'
> *pa'ū*, with a glottal stop and long *ū*, means 'moist.'

pā'ū, with a long *ā*, a long *ū*, and a glottal stop between the vowels, means 'a woman's skirt, a sarong' or 'a mat covering for a canoe.'

Some sources say that the street is *Pau*, because the canoe races on the Ala Wai Canal used to finish near this place. But others maintain that the street was named before the canal was dug.

 Niu Street

Adjoining stream to Ala Wai

Niu is the Hawaiian word for coconut (recall **I-19**, Launiu Street), the most common plant throughout the Pacific. There is also a Coconut Avenue at the foot of Diamond Head.

 McCully Street

McCully Street is 1.5 miles from the Diamond Head end of the canal.

This street is named for Lawrence McCully, owner of neighboring land and an associate justice during the reign of Kalākaua. McCully Street crosses McCully Bridge into the residential and commercial area of Mō'ili'ili (**I-3**).

Notice the group of outrigger canoes on the Diamond Head side of

WALK I ÷ ALA WAI CANAL

Hula *at King Kalākaua's 50th birthday Jubilee, 1886 (Hawai'i State Archives)*

the bridge and the benches on the *'Ewa* side.

Cross McCully—carefully and in the crosswalk, please!—then cross over the canal on the McCully Bridge to walk along the park on the *mauka* side of the canal. Find a bench, sit in the shade, rest, and enjoy the flowers, especially the hibiscus.

 Makiki Stream

Makiki Stream flows down from the mountains above Makiki (**I-3**), follows upper Kalākaua Avenue, and empties into the Ala Wai Canal just before the next bridge. In pre-canal days, this was another branch of *Pi'inaio Stream*.

From this vantage point, with your back to the beach, you can see the back of the Hawai'i Convention Center, which opened in 1998 on ten acres of land.

Cross the new, year-2000 Makiki Stream Bridge.

 Kalākaua Avenue

You may have noticed the bronze statue of King Kalākaua at the entrance to Waikīkī. This street is named in his honor and memory. Kalākaua Avenue has been the main entryway into Waikīkī since the 1800s. Known as Waikīkī Road until 1908, the roadway was unpaved; later, it was filled in with lava stones from the mountains. In 1868 a carriage traveled this route, replaced by a horse-driven tramcar in 1888, which made it possible to travel the five miles from

*King Kalākaua
(Hawai'i State Archives)*

downtown Honolulu to the foot of Diamond Head in under an hour. In 1901 electric trolleys were installed and the entry to Waikīkī was shifted to McCully Street. Today local companies have installed trolleys based on San Francisco's cable cars: Rainbow Trolley and 'Oli 'Oli Trolley, meaning 'joy or happiness.' Yes, what a fun way to ride through Waikīkī . . . reminiscent of the former transportation system!

Waikīkī trolley today

King Kalākaua, or the Merrie Monarch as he was affectionately known, was a popular and fun-loving king who ruled in a period of great turmoil for the monarchy. It was during his reign that business and money interests succeeded in usurping many powers that had traditionally belonged to the throne.

King Kalākaua is fondly remembered for his love of the Hawaiian people and their culture, and he is considered the driving force behind the renaissance of Hawaiian culture in the nineteenth century. Some of the ways he left his mark include:

- reintroducing the *hula*, which had been discouraged by the missionaries from the 1820s on.
- building beautiful 'Iolani Palace, the only palace in the United States.
- establishing Kapi'olani Park, the first major park in the islands (**VII-1**).

Before continuing, notice the 1929 date on the Kalākaua Bridge, the year the Ala Wai Canal was built.

Cross Kalākaua Avenue carefully, following the pedestrian crosswalks, and return to the *makai* side of the canal.

 Līpe'epe'e Street

Tiny Līpe'epe'e Street is best known for its unusual name, which refers to a kind of seaweed. Līpe'epe'e is a type of seaweed, or *limu* (here contracted to *lī*), which was taboo to students of the *hula* because the gods were believed 'to hide,' *pe'e*, the secrets of the *hula* from anyone who ate this particular kind of seaweed.

Ala Wai Boulevard dead-ends shortly; therefore, Līpe'epe'e Street acts as a shortcut through the area.

 Ala Wai Promenade

A promenade from Kalākaua Avenue to Ala Moana Boulevard lines both sides of the canal. Walk to the end and return on the far, *'Ewa*, side, which is more pleasant since it is removed from traffic. The promenade is bordered by Chinese banyan trees.

 McDuff Park

This is the two-mile point.

The plaque on the bench that reads "To sit or not to sit" invites you to decide.

You may walk back on the *'Ewa* side; if so, you will be walking along the back of the Hawai'i Convention Center. Notice the grand "Royal

WALK I ✢ ALA WAI CANAL

McDuff Park bench

Stairway" leading up the rear of the center. At the end of the convention center at Kalākaua, there is a Waikīkī Historic Trail marker about the canal.

This is the conclusion of Walk I. From here you may continue on to other activities:
- Walk around to the other side of the promenade;
- Walk one block '*Ewa* on Ala Moana Boulevard to Ala Moana Shopping Center; or
- If you prefer to continue walking with this book as your guide, walk one block Diamond Head to the corner of Ala Moana Boulevard and Hobron Lane to join **Walk II**: Early Hawaiian Life in Waikīkī: Taro Fields and Fishponds, Rice Fields and Duck Ponds. However, you will be walking in the reverse direction, starting from **II-21**, at the intersection of 'Ena/Kālia Road and Ala Moana Boulevard.

Walk II

• Early Hawaiian Life
in Waikīkī: *Kālia* •

Walk II

Early Hawaiian Life in Waikīkī: *Kālia*
Hawaiian Taro Fields and Fishponds
Chinese Rice Fields and Duck Ponds

🕒 **TIME:** 1.5 hours
➪ **DISTANCE:** 1 mile (1.6 kilometers)

Spirit of Hula and Land *by Kim Duffett*

THIS WALK COVERS PART OF A MUCH LARGER DISTRICT ONCE KNOWN AS *KĀLIA*, A VAST AREA OF PONDS AND FIELDS ON KĀLIA BAY THAT HAWAIIANS CALLED HOME.

Kālia was a subdivision, or *'ili*, of the *ahupua'a* 'large land division' of Waikīkī.

The name *Kālia* is translated as 'waited for.' This name derives from a Hawaiian legend based on the long wait undertaken by a young man whose beautiful wife had been wooed away by a rival Maui chieftain. We don't know whether his vigil was ever rewarded.

Until the mid-1920s, *Kālia* was a very fertile area irrigated by *Pi'inaio Stream* (**II-17**), one of three streams that flowed through Waikīkī before the Ala Wai Canal was built in the 1920s.

Taro (*kalo* in Hawaiian; the English word was borrowed from either Tahitian or Māori) is a starchy vegetable similar to the potato. Generally, all parts of this vital plant are eaten: the leaves are cooked as greens, similar to spinach; the fleshy stems and roots are eaten baked, boiled, or steamed with water to make *poi*, the staple Hawaiian food.

Two of the largest ponds, or wet fields, in *Kālia* were *Loko* (lake) *Paweo* and *Loko Ka'ihikapu*, each measuring more than twelve acres. It is believed that these complex agricultural and irrigational systems were first established by the high chief Kalamakuaakaipuholua (a.k.a. Kalamakua) in the early 1400s.

These taro fields and fishponds, and many other smaller ones, were located directly *mauka* of Kālia Road. After the arrival of the Chinese in the nineteenth century, rice fields and ponds for domesticated ducks abounded alongside the Hawaiian taro fields and fishponds. The Chinese developed rice as a major export.

The fishponds were linked to the sea by a canal controlled by a lock to retain the larger fish and to allow the smaller, undeveloped fish to go back out to sea. The lock, or stationary sluice, called *mākāhā* in Hawaiian, has been used only in Hawai'i and in the Gilbert Islands.

Legend tells us that the fishponds were inhabited by *mo'o*, twelve- to thirty-foot black-bodied deities or water serpents. Waikīkī's *mo'o* god was Kamō'ili'ili, 'pebble lizard.' (Don't worry—they all disappeared along with the ponds!)

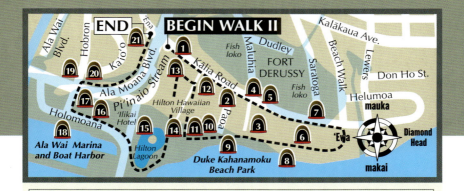

WALK II

Early Hawaiian Life in Waikīkī: *Kālia*

Hawaiian taro fields and fishponds
Chinese rice fields and duck ponds

II-1 Kālia Road
II-2 Paoa Place
II-3 Hale Koa Hotel
II-4 Maluhia Road
II-5 Kuroda Field
II-6 Fort DeRussy and Battery Randolph
  U.S. Army Museum of Hawai'i
  Chun Afong
  Alexander Joy Cartwright Jr.
II-7 Saratoga Road
  Waikīkī Post Office
II-8 Fort DeRussy Beach
II-9 Duke Kahanamoku Park
  Paoa Place
II-10 Hilton Hawaiian Village
  Niumalu Hotel
  Hawai'i Kai Beach Club Hotel
II-11 Gardens of the Hilton Hawaiian Village
  Hau Tree Beach Bar
II-12 Tapa Tower
II-13 Kālia Tower
II-14 Rainbow Mural on the Hilton Rainbow Tower
II-15 Duke Kahanamoku Lagoon/Hilton Lagoon
II-16 The Renaissance 'Ilikai Hotel and Apartments
  Ikesu Hotel and Café
II-17 *Pi'inaio Stream*
II-18 Ala Wai Marina and Boat Harbor
II-19 Hobron Lane
  Amusement Parks
II-20 *Koa* Wood in McDonald's at Discovery Bay
II-21 'Ena Road

WALK II ✧ EARLY HAWAIIAN LIFE IN WAIKĪKĪ: KĀLIA

John Papa Ī'ī, one of Hawai'i's earliest historians, mentioned a large catch of fish from *Kālia* ponds given as a tribute to Kīna'u, daughter of Kamehameha I. Another early historian, Samuel Kamakau, told of a liquor-selling establishment in a *Kālia* coconut grove.

Part of this land was deeded by King Kamehameha III to Ho'olae Paoa, Duke Kahanamoku's grandfather (**II-2** and **9**). ✤

Waikiki pre-1900 (Hawai'i State Archives)

▶ **BEGIN WALK:** *The walk begins at the intersection of Ala Moana Boulevard and Kālia Road, at the entrance to the Hilton Hawaiian Village. If you have time, take a half hour to go into the Kālia Tower of the Hilton Hawaiian Village on the corner of Ala Moana Boulevard and Kālia Road to visit the Bishop Museum annex, where you'll learn more about early Hawaiian life in Waikīkī.*

This is a loop trail, returning close to the beginning of the walk.

At the intersection of Ala Moana Boulevard and Kālia Road is a lovely bronze statue of three hula dancers: **Spirit of Hula and Land,** *by Kim Duffett. The Hawaiian inscription,* "Kaha ka 'io me nā Makani," *translates as 'The Hawk Soars with the Winds.'*

 Kālia Road

Kālia 'waited for' Road is named from the district, or *'ili,* of *Kālia.* This street is mentioned in Earl Derr Biggers's mystery novel, *The House Without a Key* (**IX-5**).

Kālia Road was moved slightly *mauka* with the construction of the newest Hale Koa Hotel building (**II-3**).

On the Hilton Hawaiian Village side of Kālia are numerous plants, many of them native. Do read the informative plaques as you walk along.

Continue along Kālia Road, crossing Paoa Place. (We will return to Paoa Place on the beach.)

 Paoa Place (Waikīkī Historic Trail marker on the beach)

The street is named for the Paoa family, Duke Kahanamoku's mother's family, who owned property near here. The land was deeded to the Duke's ancestors during the *Mahele* of 1848, the division of Hawaiian land among the rulers and the commoners. The family farmed taro and sweet potatoes here, and partook of the bounties of the sea. More about the Duke at **II-9**.

As you cross Paoa Place, look back just before the Diamond Head Tower of the Hilton, on the *'Ewa* side of Paoa: entwined banyan and coconut trees!

 Hale Koa Hotel

Hale Koa can mean either 'House of Koa Wood' or 'House of the Warrior.'

House of the Warrior is apt considering that this hotel is for use by military, or "warriors." However, *koa* is also a beautiful, strong hardwood found only in the native forests of Hawai'i. The first Hale Koa Hotel, 'Ilima, was completed in 1975 to accommodate the many soldiers and their families who get together for some R and R. The newer *'Ewa-mauka* building, Maile, opened in 1995. Over one million military personnel and their dependents get a chance to rest in this hotel on the beach! The Hale Koa boasts that it is completely self-sufficient and "not one taxpayer dollar supports the upkeep or operation."

Hale Koa Hotel

Continue on the *makai* side of Kālia Road, crossing Maluhia Road and stopping to read the Waikīkī Historic Trail marker along Kālia Road, Diamond Head of the Hale Koa Hotel.

 Maluhia Road

The street at Kuroda Field on the *mauka* side of Kālia Road is Maluhia 'peaceful' Road. Until recently, this street continued through to Kalākaua Avenue. (It still does on many maps!) On the *'Ewa* side of Maluhia Road is the green-roofed Asia-Pacific Center for Security Studies. On the Diamond Head side and on the cul-de-sac is the Fort DeRussy Army Chapel, a Hawaiian-style, low, white building.

On the grassy area at the *mauka* end of Maluhia Road stood the *Maluhia Club*, an entertainment-dance facility that was opened during World War II. This club, which accommodated twelve hundred people, marked the beginning of Fort DeRussy's transition from a military installation to a recreation center.

 Kuroda Field

Kuroda Field is located on the *mauka* side of Kālia Road. It is named in honor of the patriotism of Staff Sergeant Robert T. Kuroda, who was awarded the Medal of Honor for his actions on October 20, 1944, as a member of the 442d Regimental Combat Team. The Medal of Honor was awarded posthumously by President Clinton in 1995 as part of the fiftieth anniversary of the end of World War II. Staff Sergeant Kuroda, who is buried at the National Memorial Cemetery of the Pacific in Punchbowl, was felled by a sniper in Bruyères, France.

Some interesting facts about the 100th and 442d infantries:
- In 1944 the 442d merged with the 100th Battalion. The 100th Infantry was the first all–Japanese American combat unit.
- "Go For Broke!"—the 442d Infantry's motto, meaning "shoot the works," underscored its deserved reputation: for its size and duration of service, it was the most highly

decorated unit in military history.
• The 100th and 442d fought eight campaigns in Germany, Italy, and France. A memorial to these soldiers, Brothers in Valor, is located on the *mauka* side of Fort DeRussy, at Kalākaua Avenue (IV-2).

Fort DeRussy and Battery Randolph
U.S. Army Museum of Hawai'i
Chun Afong
6 **Alexander Joy Cartwright Jr.**

Don't look for the physical structure of a fort: there isn't—and never was—one. "Fort" simply denotes a permanent military installation of any type. The U.S. Army Museum of Hawai'i is the main attraction for tourists. However, the Hale Koa Hotel, only for members of the military and their dependents, and Fort DeRussy Beach make up the greater Fort DeRussy Armed Forces Recreation Center.

Keep in mind that this entire area is all part of Fort DeRussy: both *makai* and *mauka* of Kālia Road.

In the mid-1800s, the home of Chun Afong, the first Chinese millionaire in Hawai'i, occupied three acres along the waterfront. This was a home of opulent parties for local and foreign dignitaries. Chun Afong was known as "the merchant prince of the sandalwood mountains." Because of its great number of sandalwood trees and the Chinese love for sandalwood, Hawai'i was referred to as the "sandalwood mountains." Chun Afong was a shrewd businessman: he had his hand in real estate, rice, sugar, and even opium! However, he was

also a keen politician under King Kalākaua, having married Julia Fayerweather of the Hawaiian monarchy. The Afongs, who had sixteen children (including thirteen girls), served as character models for Jack London's "Chun Ah Chun" and for Eaton Magoon Jr.'s musical "Thirteen Daughters," which played on Broadway in 1961.

The first building preceding the structure of Fort DeRussy was the large home of Alexander Joy Cartwright Jr., a merchant who settled in Honolulu in 1849 and died in 1892. Alexander Cartwright, who was born in New York, is best known as the "father of modern baseball"; he was inducted into Cooperstown's Baseball Hall of Fame in 1934. Cartwright established baseball's first organized association, the New York Knickerbocker Base Ball Club, and established the rules and regulations of nine players and nine innings. Cartwright Field, in Makiki, 'Ewa-mauka of Waikīkī, is a baseball field named in his memory.

So how did Cartwright end up in Hawai'i? He was drawn to the gold rush in California. After tiring of the hard work, he hopped on a boat back to New York via China. He was extremely seasick and headed for land as soon as the ship reached Honolulu Harbor. The rest is history: he fell in love with the islands and stayed, bringing his wife and children two years later. He also formed Hawai'i's first fire department and became its head engineer.

The Man Who Invented Baseball, by Harold Peterson, tells the complete story of Alexander Joy Cartwright Jr.'s life. Cartwright's grave in a Nu'uanu cemetery has been visited by many baseball greats, including Babe Ruth! His son, Bruce Cartwright Sr., was one of the subdividers of Waikīkī (**VI-4**).

In 1904 the DeRussy area began to be acquired by the United States government through the U.S. Army Corps of Engineers. By 1915, and after twelve different land purchases, the government accumulated seventy-two acres. Chung Afong aside, the homes were owned mainly by people with European-sounding names: Hobron (of nearby Hobron Lane **II-19**), Waterhouse, Shaefer, McCandless, and Carter. The first military installation here was known as the Waikīkī Military Reservation, then as the Kālia Military Reservation. In 1909 it was renamed Fort DeRussy in honor of Brevet Brigadier General René Edward DeRussy (1789–1865).

General DeRussy not only fought in both the War of 1812 and the Civil War, but also designed fortifications in the New York and San Francisco harbors. Furthermore, he invented the Barbette Depressing Gun Carriage, precursor to the big, disappearing guns. Other Fort DeRussys exist in America—one in Louisiana, named after his brother, Colonel Lewis DeRussy, and the other a Union fort in Washington, D.C., named in honor of a nephew.

Fort DeRussy was originally established not as a recreation area, which is what it is today, but rather as a defense for Honolulu Harbor. Most important was Battery Randolph, the building that now houses the U.S.

Army Museum of Hawai'i. Built in 1911, this coastal auxiliary was named after Major Benjamin Harrison Randolph, who helped subdue the Philippine Insurrection of 1898–1901.

In 1969 the army attempted to knock down the walls of Battery Randolph. However, its twelve-foot, steel-reinforced cement walls and twenty-two-foot cement gun platform proved impervious to the army's efforts, and the structure is still standing. Notice the massive gun emplacements.

Kū statues by Rocky Ka'iouliokahihikolo'ehu Jensen, 1999

The five large Kū images in the style of the Hawaiian chiefdom in front of the museum were carved by Rocky Ka'iouliokahihikolo'ehu Jensen in 1999. These statues, *Na Lehua Helele'i*, 'The Scattered *Lehua* Blossoms,' commemorate the "fallen Maoli 'native' warriors of Native Hawaiian conflicts." The *lehua* blossom grows on the native Hawaiian *'ōhi'a* tree. Jensen intended for these images to transmit a feeling of power: the statues rest on a platform, representing the *heiau*, or religious temple of old.

If it's not Monday and you have some extra time, go into the U.S. Army

Museum of Hawaiʻi to see its many exhibits, especially that of early native weapons. The museum is open all other days, except New Year's and Christmas, from 10:00 A.M. to 4:15 P.M. Be sure to notice the use of native *koa* wood in the reception area and the *koa* frames throughout the museum.

The museum also houses the best-kept military secret: a reference library open to the public, with thousands of pictures and documents relating to the wars in the Pacific dating back to 1898.

Saratoga Road
Waikīkī Post Office

Saratoga Road, which runs into the U.S. Army Museum of Hawaiʻi is named for a 1880s bathhouse that operated on the beachfront near here. The Waikīkī Post Office, zip code 96815, is located on the ʻEwa side of Saratoga: a lava-faced one-story building. The U.S. Post Office issued a stamp in August 2002 commemorating Hawaiʻi's favorite sportsman, Duke Kahanamoku. The last Hawaiian figure to be featured on a U.S. stamp was King Kamehameha on a three-cent stamp in 1937.

Walk past Saratoga Road to Beach Walk, along the Diamond Head side of the Army Museum, and continue through to the beach. Complete this walk back along the beach toward the Hilton.

Fort DeRussy Beach (Waikīkī Historic Trail marker)

This beach, like all beaches in Hawaiʻi, is public property, although it serves mainly members of the military and their families staying at the Hale Koa Hotel (**II-3**). The property in this area has been owned by the United States government since 1904.

The terrace along the beach is covered with *hau* trees, which belong to the Malvaeceae (mallow) family, which includes the hibiscus. In the course of its life (one day!), the *hau* blossom displays three different colors: yellow upon opening, then bright orange, and finally red-brown when it drops. The *hau* tree had many traditional uses: its rough but lightweight wood was used for making canoe outriggers, its fiber was made into rope, and its sap and flowers were used medicinally.

Naupaka

Along the beach are groves of *naupaka*, a native beach plant found on other Pacific islands as well. Look closely for its small white flower: you will actually see a "half flower." There are many legends concerning this half blossom. One legend involves a maiden who became suspicious of her lover's faithfulness. As a test, she tore the flower in two and gave him one of the halves, telling him to bring back a complete flower as proof of his love. Her lover was unsuccessful.

Another legend involves a related

mountain plant that bears an identical flower but has drastically different leaves. In this legend, a Hawaiian *Romeo and Juliet*, lovers who had been forbidden to marry because of their different backgrounds and social classes, decided to die together. The Hawaiian gods turned the woman into the *naupaka kahakai* (by the sea) and the man into the *naupaka kuahiwi* (mountain), joining their love in spirit.

Some of the other plants along the beach are endemic (found only in Hawai'i), such as *'ākia* shrubs, and others are indigenous (also found in other places in the Pacific), such as the *'ilima* plant, with its small yellow-orange flower, the size of a nickel.

At one time there were diving platforms floating offshore that were fun to swim to, climb on, rest on a while, and then dive off of!

**Duke Kahanamoku Park
(Waikīkī Historic Trail marker)
Paoa Place**

The sign designating this as Duke Kahanamoku Park is on the *mauka* side of the park.

Duke Paoa Kahanamoku (1890–1968), Hawai'i's best-known sportsman, was affectionately known as "the Duke." In 1912 he won an Olympic gold medal for the 100-meter freestyle and a silver for free relay; in 1920, two golds: one in freestyle and one in free relay; and in 1924, a silver in free relay. In 1966, he was the first person to be inducted into the Surfing Hall of Fame. It is said that over ten thousand people attended his funeral off the shores of Waikīkī. The International Surfing

Duke Kahanamoku statue (IX-17)

Championship continues to be held in his honor and memory.

His name is explained as follows:
• Duke Kahanamoku was named for his father, who, in turn, had been named by Princess Pauahi Bishop in commemoration of the 1869 visit to Hawai'i of Alfred Ernest Albert, Duke of Edinburgh.
• *Paoa* means 'fragrant' and was the name of his mother's family.
• *Kahanamoku* translates as 'island work.'

The Duke spent most of his youth here in *Kālia* with the Paoas. The Hilton Hawaiian Village sits on most of the twenty acres the family once owned. One of the Duke's sixteen-foot surfboards is on display at the Bishop Museum annex in the Kālia Tower of the Hilton Hawaiian Village.

Notice all the interesting plants in the park: mesquite, papaya trees, banana plants, ti plants (both red and green), even sugarcane. And one small native *koa* tree grows along the *mauka* wall; its leaves are crescent shaped, similar to eucalyptus leaves. *Koa* grows to great heights in the mountains; this may be the sole *koa* tree in Waikīkī!

Hilton Hawaiian Village Niumalu Hotel
Hawai'i Kai Beach Club Hotel

Relax on one of the benches in front of the lava fountain. Lava is the native stone of Hawai'i. Many buildings have been, and continue to be, built with lava stone.

Before the parade of hotels began on this property, the area was replete with pools and ponds.

In the early 1890s, the earliest commercial structure on this beach was a bathhouse-boarding house called *Old Waikīkī*. By the early 1900s, it had become more of a boarding house, first under the ownership of John and Eliza Cassidy, who called their hotel *Cassidy's-at-the-Beach*, and later as the *Pierpont Hotel*. Several bathhouses and boarding houses in Waikīkī were first established as annexes to downtown Honolulu hotels. In 1922 J. F. Child used this building as an annex for his downtown hotel. However, in the mid-1920s, this property and several other boarding houses in the immediate area were bought up by Afong Heen, a local Chinese merchant and architect. Heen renovated, enlarged, and turned these structures into the first large hotel on this site: the *Niumalu Hotel*, 'shade of the coconut tree.' The name lives on at the Niumalu Restaurant in the Kālia Tower.

The *Hawai'i Kai Beach Club Hotel*, built by Henry Kaiser (as in Kaiser Permanente Medical Care Program and Kaiser Aluminum) in 1951, was the next hotel in this area. Portions of that hotel survived until the last of the Hilton Towers was built in 2001.

In 1956 the *Hawai'i Kai Hotel* was purchased by Conrad Hilton, and expansion to the present-day Hilton Hawaiian Village was begun. Today it includes six towers on twenty-two acres of land.

Come back in the evening for the fabulous fireworks display.

Gardens of the Hilton Hawaiian Village
Hau Tree Beach Bar

Located right off the beach is the Hau Tree Beach Bar, loaded with *hau* growing everywhere! When the first edition of this book was published in 1983, this bar's name was a misnomer: the *hau* tree had been removed due to disease. But as you can see, the *hau* has returned prodigiously and its branches and leaves cover the entire roof. The *hau* tree has been replicated as a carving over the bar.

Do walk around the gardens of the Hilton, reading the plaques, to learn about the local plants, both endemic (native only in Hawai'i and nowhere else in the world) and indigenous.

Tapa Tower

The building on the Diamond Head side of the Hilton Hawaiian Village is the thirty-five-story Tapa Tower. Here, tapa refers to the pattern carved on the building. Walk through the lobby, stopping to learn about real tapa—or Hawaiian *kapa*—in the more than one dozen glass coffee tables. The Hawaiian word is related to the

Tapa

Tahitian and Marquesan form, from which the English word was borrowed. (Compare English *taboo*—from Tongan *tapu*—and Hawaiian *kapu*.) Tapa is the fabric made from the bark of the *wauke* 'paper mulberry' tree. Tapa has been used for clothing and bedding. The term also refers to the geometric patterns made by wooden beaters applied to the cloth. To see more fabrics and beaters, visit the Bishop Museum's installation in the Kālia Tower.

Be sure to view the large glass display case of Hawai'i's *kapa* artist Puanani Van Dorpe. Starting in the 1970s, she revived the ancient art of tapa making and is considered to be a Living Treasure of Hawai'i.

Walk through the Tapa Tower toward the Kālia Tower, stopping in the Tapa Tower lobby to view the old photographs in the display cases on the Diamond Head wall and the two bronze statues. One is of Alfred Apaka, a very talented and popular singer and ukulele player, who performed at the Hilton Hawaiian Village. The other is of 'Iolani Luahine,

one of Hawai'i's greatest *hula* dancers, who performed here in the 1950s. Both statues are by local artist Kim Duffett.

If you visited Waikīkī between the '60s and '80s, you may find yourself looking for the *Buckminster Fuller Dome* (known locally as *"the Dome"*), built in 1957 of Kaiser Aluminum and the 1980s home of Don Ho. It has been replaced by the Hilton's newest building, the Kālia Tower. It was at *the Dome* where Hawai'i saw its first color TV program.

Tapa Tower

 Kālia Tower

This newest of the Hilton Hawaiian Village towers is named for the local area, *Kālia*. The waterfalls in

Statue with evening sky

WALK II ✦ EARLY HAWAIIAN LIFE IN WAIKĪKĪ: KĀLIA

the lobby are spectacular and reminiscent of true waterfalls in the mountainous areas of inland Hawai'i. (Be sure to hike to Mānoa Falls, in the valley beyond the University of Hawai'i at Mānoa.) The lobby is resplendent with lush carpets of flower designs and murals of Hawaiian women by island artist Yvonne Cheng. The Niumalu Restaurant is named after an early hotel that stood on the grounds of the Hilton.

Princess Bernice Pauahi Bishop (1831–1884) (Hawai'i State Archives)

An annex of the Bishop Museum is located in this tower. Do visit, especially if you don't have time to go to the main museum in Kalihi. The Bishop Museum was founded in 1889 by Charles Reed Bishop in memory of his wife, Princess Bernice Pauahi Bishop (1831–1884), the last successor of the royal Kamehameha family. There is an incredible array of activities and displays: tour the native plants in the gardens, make Hawaiian crafts, learn about the early Polynesians and Hawaiians, see Duke Kahanamoku's surfboard, discover what the Hawaiians ate, and hear authentic Hawaiian chants and music.

Walk back toward the beach, passing the Hilton Rainbow Tower.

Rainbow Mural on the Hilton Rainbow Tower

The Hilton Rainbow Tower is known for its two 286-foot ceramic tile murals, one on the *mauka* 'mountain' side of the building, the other on the *makai* 'ocean' side. When these murals were created in 1968 by Millard Sheets (1907–1990), it was claimed that they were the tallest murals in the world. More than eight thousand ceramic tiles were used in each mural.

This mural portrays two separate rainbows rather than the double rainbow often seen in Hawai'i after a light rainfall. Double rainbows consist of a bright main rainbow below a fainter outside rainbow. The outside rainbow is always a mirror image of the main rainbow, and its colors are in reverse order. Notice that in this mural the colors of both rainbows are in the same order. Perhaps Mr. Sheets didn't spend enough time in Hawai'i!

Rainbows are often visible from Waikīkī looking *mauka* (toward the mountains) in the afternoon (**I-3**). Look carefully at the next rainbow you see—it may well be a double one!

The Hawaiian inscription beneath the *makai* rainbow is translated as:

> DEDICATED TO THE PEOPLE
> AND SPIRIT OF HAWAII

If you love rainbows, be sure to read *The Rainbow Goblins*, by Ul de Rico.

On the beach at the lagoon, this walk overlaps with the beginning of **Walk IX**, Beach Walk, which goes in the opposite direction, toward Diamond Head.

Walk 'Ewa along the beach, around the lagoon, and up the spiral walkway to the back of the 'Ilikai Hotel. Stop at the Waikīkī Historic Trail marker.

Duke Kahanamoku Lagoon/Hilton Lagoon

This lagoon is named in honor and memory of Hawai'i's favorite sportsman, "the Duke."

The Renaissance 'Ilikai Hotel and Apartments
Ikesu Hotel and Café

A Japanese nightclub and teahouse, the *Ikesu*, preceded the 'Ilikai on this site. The Japanese word *ikesu* means 'holding pond for fish,' perhaps so named because of the large Hawaiian fishponds in this area.

The 'Ilikai, 'surface of the sea,' includes a large hotel and an apartment complex for permanent and semipermanent residents. Be sure to have coffee at the Canoes at the 'Ilikai Café overlooking the Ala Wai Marina, especially in the late afternoon when the sun drops into the ocean. Look for the legendary "green flash," a momentary burst of bright green light

Ala Wai Marina boats

on the upper surface of the sun—the result of atmospheric refraction.

Famed science fiction writer Jules Verne described the green flash:

> It will be a green ray of such a fabulous beauty that no painter could produce it upon his palette, a green that nature with all her varied vegetation and all her colored waters, no matter how limpid, has never equaled. If there is a color called green in paradise, it is perhaps this green, which is without doubt, the true green of hope. Legend declares that happiness will be the portion of those who behold this spectacle. Those who do not know what happiness is should search after the green ray.

May you find eternal happiness!

Pi'inaio Stream

Until the construction of the Ala Wai Canal in the 1920s, *Pi'inaio Stream* **(I-24)** ran through this area and emptied into the ocean between the Hilton Lagoon/Duke Kahanamoku Lagoon and the 'Ilikai Hotel. *Pi'inaio Stream* was one of the three major streams that fed Waikīkī's intricate irrigation system. The *Pi'inaio* flowed down from the mountains, through the valleys, into Waikīkī, and out to the Pacific Ocean.

Unlike *'Āpuakēhau* and *Kuekaunahi* streams, which flowed directly into the Pacific Ocean, *Pi'inaio* ended further inland and became a muddy delta to the ocean. This is what made the area ripe for fishponds and taro fields for the Hawaiians, and then duck ponds and rice fields for the Chinese at the end of the nineteenth century.

When the Ala Wai Canal was built to deliberately divert those rivers, Waikīkī's ponds and fields dried up, and with them vanished the traditional Hawaiian way of life in Waikīkī.

Today's Makiki Stream most likely follows the flow of the ancient Pi'inaio Stream.

Ala Wai Marina and Boat Harbor

Harbor sunset

Walk out across the 'Ilikai deck toward the ocean and the Ala Wai Marina and Boat Harbor, where there is a ten-year wait for a slip. The marina was constructed following the dredging of the Ala Wai Canal in the 1920s, but this area had been used by fishermen long before.

The Ala Wai Marina is home to several yacht clubs, including the Hawai'i Yacht Club, Waikīkī Yacht Club, and the Ala Wai Yacht Club, and over seven hundred sailboats. The Hawai'i Yacht Club has been in existence since 1901. The Waikīkī Yacht Club, with a pool, restaurant, and bar, is the largest; Duke Kahanamoku was one of its founding members. The smaller Ala Wai Yacht Club is located across the mouth of the canal near Ala Moana Beach Park.

Friday nights after 5:00 P.M., the Beer Can Races bring out the competitive nature in our sailors. Come join the fun!

The majestic Wai'anae mountain range looms 'Ewa.

Take the escalator down the 'Ewa side of the 'Ilikai Hotel, and cross Ala Moana Boulevard at Hobron Lane.

Hobron Lane Amusement Parks

Hobron Lane is named for the Hobron brothers, Captain Coit Hobron and Thomas H. Hobron, who lived in Hawai'i during the days of the monarchy and owned property near here.

In the 1920s and 1930s, this district was a place of great fun, including *Aloha Amusement Park* and later *Waikīkī Park*. The entrance arcade was based on that at San Francisco's Palace of Fine Arts.

Kaiser Hospital was once located 'Ewa of this intersection. Now known as Kaiser Moanalua Medical Center, it moved to a location near the airport to make room for the Hawai'i Prince Hotel and its five-story cascading fountain.

Koa Wood in McDonald's at Discovery Bay

Discovery Bay, the twin-tower condominium on the *mauka*-Diamond Head corner of Hobron Lane and Ala Moana Boulevard, houses McDonald's on the ground floor. Go inside to appreciate the dazzling use of

Hawai'i's native *koa* wood in the spectacular paneled walls and ceiling. Also admire the *koa*-framed photographs of old Hawai'i. *Koa* is an endemic medium hardwood also used in artistic carvings; it is the largest of the native trees of Hawai'i.

Continue along Kālia Road, but notice that across Ala Moana Boulevard, the street's name changes to 'Ena Road.

 'Ena Road

The *'Ewa-mauka* extension of Kālia Road is 'Ena Road, named for the son of John 'Ena, a Chinese merchant, and the Chiefess Kaikilani. The 'Enas owned land in this area. John 'Ena, the son, was a member of Queen Lili'uokalani's staff.

This is the conclusion of Walk II. If you still have energy, walk around this neighborhood known as the Hobron Lane District. It is Waikīkī's most densely populated residential area, consisting mainly of apartment buildings and condominiums.

King Kamehameha's residence (Hawai'i State Archives)

Walk III
· Early Royalty ·

Walk III
Early Royalty
Central Waikīkī, along the beach

🕒 **TIME:** 0.5 hour to 2 hours, depending on your imagination!

⇨ **DISTANCE:** 0.5 mile (0.8 kilometers)

Fisherman in a three-man canoe (Hawai'i State Archives)

THIS WALK COMPRESSES HUNDREDS OF YEARS OF HAWAIIAN HISTORY INTO A HALF-HOUR WALK. You will need to use your imagination to contemplate what might have been, for nothing remains from the years before Western contact save the reminders contained in two street names: Helumoa Road (**III-1**) and Uluniu Avenue (**III-9**). In about the year 1400, O'ahu King Mā'ilikūkahi moved his capital from 'Ewa to Waikīkī. Waikīkī reigned supreme for almost four hundred years, until Kamehameha I moved the capital from Waikīkī to Honolulu in 1809 and then to the Big Island in 1812.

Kamehameha I united the islands in 1810. Had he stayed in Waikīkī, Waikīkī would have been the capital of all the islands. As it stands, Waikīkī must be content with having been the capital of O'ahu for four hundred years. ❀

▶ **BEGIN WALK:** *This walk begins at the corner of Helumoa Road and Beach Walk.*

Helumoa Road runs parallel to Kālia Road, one block mauka *of the Halekūlani Hotel.*

 Helumoa Road
1 *Helumoa*

Helumoa, 'chicken scratch,' Road is the only remnant of an important place in ancient Hawaiian times. *Helumoa*, where Hawaiian royalty lived, was located from here to the beach; it is thought to have extended from the present-day Royal Hawaiian Hotel (**IX-9**) to the Outrigger Hotel (**IX-10**).

The earliest features of *Helumoa* were the homes of the local chiefs, followed by the royal residences of most of the Hawaiian monarchy from Kamehameha on. Other structures at *Helumoa* included a *heiau*, 'religious structure,' and an athletic field, based on artifacts found in the area.

There are several stories about this place. According to one legend, Kākuhihewa, chief of O'ahu in the sixteenth century, was playing Hawaiian games here one day when a legendary phantom rooster, Ka'auhelemoa, suddenly landed in front of him and began to scratch the earth. Just as suddenly, the rooster disappeared. Kākuhihewa directed his men to plant a coconut in the exact spot where Ka'auhelemoa had scratched. This coconut came to be

❀ 32 ❀

WALK III
Early Royalty

Central Waikīkī, along the beach

NINE WALKS THROUGH TIME

III-1	Helumoa Road
	Helumoa
III-2	Kawehewehe
III-3	Puaali'ili'i (or Pua'ali'ili'i)
	King's Park and Grove
III-4	Heiau 'Āpuakēhau
III-5	Kahuamokomoko Athletic Field
III-6	'Āpuakēhau Stream
III-7	Hamohamo
III-8	Ulukou
III-9	Uluniu
	Uluniu Avenue
	King's Coconut Grove
III-10	Kalehuawehe

known as Helumoa and, in turn, supported a grove of several thousand coconut trees. Helumoa was always the tallest and strongest.

Another legend tells of chickens scratching the ground for maggots in the shallow graves of sacrificial victims from the nearby *heiau*, ʻĀpuakēhau (**III-4**).

Take a few minutes to walk into the *makai* 'oceanside' lobby of the Ohana Edgewater Hotel on the corner of Helumoa and Beach Walk to view the photos of old Waikīkī and Hawaiʻi.

Continue toward the beach on Lewers, then walk Diamond Head along Kālia Road (**Walk II**) to the right-of-way through to the beach.

Kawehewehe (Waikīkī Historic Trail marker)

Waikīkī c. 1885 (Hawaiʻi State Archives)

The beach and waters fronting today's Halekūlani were called *Kawehewehe*, 'the removal,' by the ancient Hawaiians. According to legend, sick and injured people were brought here for curative bathing treatments. Often, a seaweed *lei* was worn, to be removed and left behind as a symbolic request that one's sins, believed to be the cause of illness, be forgiven.

Modern-day Hawaiians continue to use the ocean waters therapeutically.

Kawehewehe can also mean 'the opening in the reef,' referring to the reef entrance, offshore channel, and tide pool in this area.

Walk along the beach toward Diamond Head to the water's edge in front of the Outrigger Waikīkī Hotel.

Puaaliʻiliʻi or Puaʻaliʻiliʻi King's Park and Grove

Try to imagine this area 100 years ago: the king's home of lava stone, an open religious structure, a sports field, a stream, and more royal homes on the other side of the stream. As a royal residence, the area was *kapu*, or taboo, to commoners (yes, you and me!).

Depending on where the glottal stop (the sound between the two vowel sounds in *uh-oh*) is placed, there can be two entirely different meanings for this place name: *pua aliʻiliʻi* means 'flower of the exalted royalty,' but *puaʻa liʻiliʻi* means 'little pig'! The most likely meaning of this area's name is the first one, since this seems more appropriate for a royal residence. However, the pig was formerly held sacred, coming down through history in legends. This double meaning may be deliberate, based on the *kaona*, double or hidden meaning, in Hawaiian.

The following royal homes were located in *Helumoa* on the *mauka* gardens of the Royal Hawaiian Hotel:
• King Kamehameha I's stone house. He called his home here *Kūihelani*, 'heavenly spear of Kū'—the war god. He lived here off and on from 1795 to 1809.

EARLY ROYALTY ✣ **WALK III**

Kamehameha V's summer house (Hawai'i State Archives)

- King Kamehameha III's home in the 1830s. This was a Western-style one-bedroom house.
- Kamehameha V's home. He reigned from 1863 to 1872. His thatch-roofed lava stone house was also referred to as the *Lama* House because of its native *lama* wood (an endemic kind of ebony).

Whatever the actual layout of those ancient sites may have been, the area, no doubt, presented a striking panorama from the ocean.

There would have been several reasons for making this site ideal for a royal home: the neighboring freshwater stream; the area's elevation and natural irrigation system; Waikīkī's suitability as a safe harbor for war canoes; immediate availability of food staples, such as fish and fowl, and taro, coconut, and ti plants (See **Walk II**, Early Hawaiian Life in Waikīkī); and the beauty of the beach and its surroundings.

According to legend, O'ahu chiefs, including Kamehameha I (a.k.a. Kamehameha the Great) lived in *Helumoa* for years. Kamehameha

moved his court here from the Big Island, including his favorite wife, Ka'ahumanu, in 1795. With Waikīkī as the capital of O'ahu, he remained there off and on until 1809, one year before he unified the islands.

Kamehameha I then moved to downtown Honolulu, to today's intersection of Queen Street and Nimitz Highway. In 1812 he returned to his home in Kona on the island of Hawai'i, where he remained until his death in 1819. Since Kamehameha's descendants continued living on this beach, the area came to be known, not surprisingly, as the King's Park and Grove.

King Kalākaua and Queen Kapi'olani's residence (Hawai'i State Archives)

✣ 35 ✣

Heiau ʻĀpuakēhau

Heiau ʻĀpuakēhau, a religious structure, was located ʻEwa of the Royal Hawaiian Hotel. The name is taken from the nearby *ʻĀpuakēhau Stream*.

Human sacrifice (Hawaiʻi State Archives)

This *heiau* was rectangular and very large, approximately 130 feet by 70 feet, with 4- to 8-foot walls on three sides, the open side parallel with the shoreline.

A *heiau* is a sacred stone temple to which access to commoners was strictly limited. There were different types of *heiau*: agricultural *heiau*, for economic needs or husbandry, to ensure the livelihood of the people; and sacrificial *heiau*, usually as war temples. Most *heiau* were damaged in 1819 when the Hawaiian religion and *kapu* system were challenged by Kamehameha II.

Soon after the death of Kamehameha I in 1819, his wives and son (Kamehameha II) set about to abolish the ways of their traditional religion. This did not come about overnight: Kaʻahumanu, Kamehameha's favorite wife, had already challenged and, thereby, had broken the *kapu* not only of eating with men, but also eating food (bananas) forbidden to women. This change opened the way for the Christian religion that was brought to Hawaiʻi by the missionaries the following year, 1820.

Yes, there were human sacrifices in Hawaiʻi, but the Hawaiians were not cannibals. One of the most famous people to have been sacrificed here was Kauhiakama, the high chief of Maui, in 1610. His death was avenged 170 years later by Kahekili of Maui with another sacrifice at *Heiau Papaʻenaʻena* on the slope of Diamond Head (**VIII-14**).

Kahuamokomoko Athletic Field

Kahuamokomoko, 'sports field for boxing,' was probably located on the site of the Royal Hawaiian Hotel. Game stones, *ʻulu maika*, stone disks used in a game similar to bowling, have been unearthed there. Boxing and a form of bowling were popular sports among Hawaiians.

If you would like to participate in authentic Hawaiian games, be sure to visit the Bishop Museum in the Kālia Tower of the Hilton Hawaiian Village. Most afternoons, Hawaiian games are set up for all to play. You, too, can play *ʻulu maika*, just like the Hawaiians!

ʻĀpuakēhau Stream

ʻĀpuakēhau Stream, a wide, freshwater stream, flowed on the other side of the sports field. Until the 1920s, when this river was diverted by the Mānoa-Pālolo Drainage Canal (**I-17**) to create the Ala Wai Canal, *ʻĀpuakēhau Stream* came down from the Koʻolau mountain range, flowed into this area, under today's Outrigger Waikīkī Hotel, and out to the ocean. This was the middle of three rivers that flowed through Waikīkī.

'Āpuakēhau means 'basket of dew.' The name for this stream may derive from the vast quantities of ti, *hau*, and palm plants that lined its banks. The royalty rinsed their bodies in this cool, freshwater stream after swimming and surfing in the ocean.

Hau belongs to the Malvaeceae (mallow) family, which includes the hibiscus. In the course of its life (one day!), the *hau* blossom displays three different colors: yellow upon opening, then bright orange, and finally red-brown when it drops. The *hau* tree had many traditional uses: its rough but lightweight wood was used for making canoe outriggers; its fibers were made into rope; and its sap and flowers were used medicinally. There are still many areas of *hau* along the beach today. Just look for a hibiscus-like flower.

Hamohamo

The area from the Ala Wai Canal to the ocean, between *'Āpuakēhau* and *Kuekaunahi* streams (**IX-18**) was known as *Hamohamo*, 'soothing' or 'rub gently.' Its name may have referred to the water lapping at the shoreline. This area was the home of Hawai'i's last reigning monarch, Queen Lili'uokalani (**V-10**).

Ulukou

Ulukou, '*kou* tree grove,' surrounded the royal residence that extended from *'Āpuakēhau Stream* in front of the present-day Moana Hotel. The *kou* tree is found in the Pacific Islands. *Kou* wood is most useful, often carved into bowls, cups, and dishes.

Many O'ahu chiefs made their homes in *Ulukou*, making Waikīkī the capital of O'ahu for four hundred years!

Some of these chiefs were:

- 'Aikanaka, 'man eater,' a ruling chief.
- Kahekili, a conquering chief from Maui, who invaded Waikīkī and spent his final days here at the end of the eighteenth century.
- Kalanikūpule, Kahekili's son, who lived here until being conquered by Kamehameha I in 1795.

Uluniu
Uluniu Avenue
King's Coconut Grove

Uluniu, 'coconut grove,' referred to a grove of several thousand coconut trees that surrounded King Kalākaua's residence here. Kalākaua's primary residence, however, was 'Iolani Palace in downtown Honolulu. Be sure to visit the only royal palace in the United States of America!

Ceremonies at 'Iolani Palace, August 12, 1898, when Hawai'i changed from Republic to the Territory of Hawai'i (Hawai'i State Archives)

WALK III ✦ EARLY ROYALTY

Surfboard pre-1900 (Hawai'i State Archives)

The coconut trees along the beach today are descendants of trees from the time of the early Hawaiian monarchs. During his visit in 1866, Mark Twain referred to the coconut trees as "the King's Coconut Grove."

The land and home were left to Prince Kūhiō, who lived here until his death in 1922. The land was left to Kapi'olani Medical Center for Women and Children, named in memory and honor of Queen Kapi'olani.

Uluniu Avenue, Diamond Head of the twin-tower Hyatt Regency, commemorates that famous grove.

 Kalehuawehe

Hawaiians, especially the royalty of old, traditionally enjoyed the fine surf of Waikīkī. Though its exact location is no longer known, one of the favorite surfing areas was named *Kalehuawehe*, 'the removed or untied *lei lehua*.'

There are two Hawaiian legends associated with the name *Kalehuawehe*. According to one legend, the name originated when a young chief from Mānoa (**I-3**) removed his *lei lehua* and gave it to the daughter of Chief Kākuhihewa. Until then, only the princess had been permitted to surf there, but she broke the *kapu* by accepting the *lei*.

The other legend tells of a Hawaiian "Robin Hood," Pīkoi, who went to Waikīkī wearing a *lei lehua*. He asked a surfing princess if he could borrow her surfboard, which, of course, she refused, as the board was *kapu*. The legend does a flip-flop, however, and they surfed anyway after Pīkoi gave the princess his *lei!*

Kalehuawehe may have been in the general area of the Moana Hotel or as far away as Castle's, Diamond Head of here (**VIII-8** and **9**).

This is the end of **Walk III**. If you would like to continue walking through history, follow this tour with **Walk V**, Last Days of the Monarchy, which begins at the Princess Ka'iulani Hotel, one block *'Ewa* of Uluniu, off Kalākaua Avenue.

Other possible continuations from this point are:
• **Walk VII**, Kapi'olani Park and Honolulu Zoo; or
• **Walk VIII**, Foot of Diamond Head.

Walk IV
· Miracle Mile ·

Waikīkī Gateway Park

Walk IV
Miracle Mile: Waikīkī from the 1930s through the 1950s

🕐 **TIME:** 45 minutes
⇨ **DISTANCE:** 1 mile (1.6 kilometers)

THIS WALK PROCEEDS ALONG WAIKĪKĪ'S "MIRACLE MILE," KALĀKAUA AVENUE. TRADITIONALLY, THE "MIRACLE" REFERS TO THE INCREDIBLE TRANSFORMATION THIS AREA HAS EXPERIENCED FROM THE TIME OF THE HAWAIIAN ROYALTY TO THE PRESENT. I call it the Miracle Mile because of the few beautiful buildings that still remain—Gump's (**IV-4**) and the Waikīkī Theater (**IV-7**)—and the Charlot frescoes (**IV-17**). 🎤

▶ BEGIN WALK: *This tour starts at the park on the corner of Kalākaua Avenue and Kūhiō Avenue, and returns on the* makai *side of Kalākaua. This can be a loop trail. As you walk along Kalākaua Avenue, notice the Victorian street lamps and the hanging flower baskets, evoking bygone times.*

1 David Kalākaua Park and Kalākaua Avenue
Waikīkī Gateway Park
Kūhiō Avenue

The park and the main avenue through Waikīkī are named after one of the last rulers of Hawai'i: King David La'amea Kalākaua. Waikīkī Gateway Park marks the entrance to Waikīkī.

The street on the *makai* side of the statue, Kalākaua Avenue, has been the main entryway into Waikīkī since the 1800s. Originally known as Waikīkī Road, it was unpaved and later lined with lava rocks from the mountains. In 1868 a small bus traveled this route; it was replaced by a horse-drawn trolley in 1888, which made it possible to travel the five miles from downtown Honolulu to the foot of Diamond Head in under an hour. In 1901 electric trolleys were installed. Today, reproduction trolleys, Waikīkī Trolley and 'Oli 'Oli Trolley, meaning 'joy' or 'happiness,' run here. What a fun way to ride through Waikīkī ... reminiscent of the former transportation system!

Before you stands a larger-than-life statue of King David La'amea Kalākaua, who lived from 1836 to 1891 and reigned from 1874 until his death. His Hawaiian names are significant: La'amea means 'sacred one' and Kalākaua means 'the day of battle.' He was followed by Queen Lili'uokalani, who ruled only two years before the "provisional government" took over.

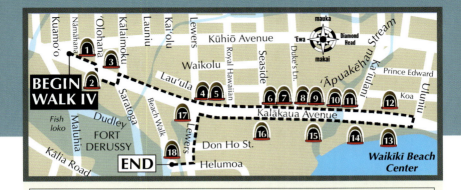

WALK IV
Miracle Mile

Waikīkī from the 1930s through the 1950s

IV-1 David Kalākaua Park and Kalākaua Avenue
Waikīkī Gateway Park
Kūhiō Avenue
IV-2 Brothers in Valor Memorial Park
IV-3 King Kalākaua Plaza
IV-4 *Gump's* (Gump Building)
2200 Kalākaua Avenue
IV-5 Waikīkī Walk at the Galleria
IV-6 Waikīkī Business Plaza
IV-7 Waikīkī Theater
IV-8 Duke's Lane
IV-9 Macy's Department Store (former *Liberty House*)
IV-10 International Market Place
Kaluaokau
IV-11 Princess Ka'iulani Shops
IV-12 Hyatt Regency Waikīkī Hotel
Peacock Residence
IV-13 Police Station
Waikīkī Inn and Tavern
Waikīkī Bowling Alley
Pualeilani
IV-14 Moana Hotel
Sheraton Moana
Surfrider Hotel
IV-15 Outrigger Waikīkī Hotel
Outrigger Canoe Club's Original Location
Duke's Restaurant
IV-16 Royal Hawaiian Shopping Center
IV-17 First Hawaiian Bank
Jean Charlot Fresco Murals
IV-18 Ohana Edgewater Hotel

WALK IV ✥ MIRACLE MILE

The statue of King Kalākaua commemorates the 100th anniversary of the arrival of Japanese sugar

Kalākaua statue

plantation workers in Hawai'i. This is the reason the inscription is in both English and Japanese. When Kalākaua visited Japan in 1881 as part of his world tour, he signed an agreement to bring Japanese contract laborers to Hawai'i. Between 1885, when the first Japanese workers began to arrive, and 1924, 220,000 Japanese came.

King Kalākaua is fondly remembered for his love of the Hawaiian people and their culture. He is considered the driving force behind the renaissance of Hawaiian culture in the nineteenth century:
- He reintroduced the *hula*, which had been banned by the missionaries after their arrival in 1820.
- He built beautiful 'Iolani Palace, the only royal palace in the United States.
- He established Kapi'olani Park, the first major park in the islands (**VII-1**).

Kalākaua and Robert Louis Stevenson, the famous author who was enamored with Hawai'i, were often seen together. Stevenson considered Kalākaua a "cultured intellectual of unusual mental powers." King Kalākaua was only distantly related to Kamehameha I through a common ancestor. The ruling line shifted to the Kalākaua lineage when the Kamehameha line failed to produce an heir to the throne, and Kalākaua was elected monarch.

The Merrie Monarch, as Kalākaua was affectionately known, was a popular and fun-loving king who ruled in a period of great turmoil for the monarchy. It was during his reign that business and money interests succeeded in usurping many powers that had traditionally belonged to the throne.

Kūhiō Avenue (on the *mauka* side of the statue) is named for Prince Jonah Kūhiō Kalaniana'ole, who lived from 1871 to 1922. Prince Kūhiō's mother was sister to Queen Kapi'olani (**VII-1**, Kapi'olani Park); his father was king of Kaua'i. He served as a delegate to the United States Congress and was instrumental in enacting the 1920 Hawaiian Homes Commission Act, which granted two hundred thousand acres of land to native Hawaiians. Kūhiō's death marked the end of the royal realm at Waikīkī. The road through East Honolulu and to Hanauma Bay and beyond, Kalaniana'ole Highway, is also named after him, as is Kūhiō Beach Park, where there is a statue of him (**IX-16**). Kūhiō Day is celebrated on March 26.

Continue Diamond Head along Kalākaua Avenue, past Nick's Fishmarket restaurant in the Waikīkī Gateway Hotel. (But do come back at night for delicious local fish. The fresh *'ōpakapaka* is the author's all-time favorite. Try it!)

Refer to **Walk I** for the history of the street names along Kalākaua Avenue. Notice the bike sculptures doubling as bike stands.

Cross Kalākaua Avenue to the park on the other side.

 Brothers in Valor Memorial Park

Brothers in Valor Memorial

This poignant sculpture by Honolulu artist Bumpei Akaji, a 442d Infantry veteran, honors World War II veterans. The monument includes a time capsule with the names of soldiers killed in action. Walk around, sit for a while, and contemplate the power of these soldiers who fought for our freedom. The concept for this memorial originated with Judy M. Weightman (1941–1998), a University of Hawai'i at Mānoa law professor. She interviewed Japanese soldiers who helped liberate the Dachau concentration camp; a plaque in her memory is located nearby.

This memorial is aptly situated here: this is Fort DeRussy land. The U.S. Army Museum of Hawai'i, located *makai* of here (**II-6**), is open to the public.

Cross back to the *mauka* side of Kalākaua Avenue where Kālaimoku Street becomes Saratoga Road. The walk continues for several blocks, then crosses back again to the *makai* side to return through the Royal Hawaiian Shopping Center.

 King Kalākaua Plaza

This newest of the Waikīkī shopping areas replaces a string of smaller shops similar to those Diamond Head of this plaza. The building on the corner has a particularly distinctive roof.

Continue along Kalākaua Avenue to the corner of Lewers Street. Notice the rainbow shower trees.

 Gump's **(Gump Building)**
2200 Kalākaua Avenue

Gump Building

The white building with the blue-tiled roof on the corner of Lewers and Kalākaua housed one of Waikīkī's earliest retail stores, and it remains one of the most beautiful buildings in Waikīkī. This stately, elegant structure dates to 1929, when it opened its doors as a branch of the San Francisco art dealer S. & G. Gump, a firm itself dating to 1861. Today, this stunning building houses a popular retail store. Notice the fine building features:

imperial blue-tiled roof, dark-stained imported teak wood exterior, antique copper gutters and window frames, and iron railing. When *Gump's* opened to its "steamboat set" clientele in 1929, the interior walls were carpeted.

 Waikīkī Walk at the Galleria

Another large shopping center on this street! However, this one has interesting Hawaiian elements along "Waikīkī Walk," evoking a 1920s ocean liner. *Hula* shows are scheduled in the evenings.

Cross Royal Hawaiian Avenue, which, if followed toward the beach, does lead to the Royal Hawaiian Hotel. For now, continue along Kalākaua, crossing Seaside, so named for the *Waikīkī Seaside Hotel*, which stood on the site of the Royal Hawaiian Hotel from 1894 to 1927.

 Waikīkī Business Plaza

This building houses the Waikīkī Theater (next stop), the Don Ho show, and Top of Waikīkī, a revolving restaurant, on its twenty-first floor.

On the corner is a two-story ceramic mural of fish swimming against the current by Robert Flint. (Flint also created a lovely ceramic mural of a native Hawaiian butterfly at the entrance to Gilmore Hall at the University of Hawai'i at Mānoa.)

 Waikīkī Theater

A true miracle on the "Miracle Mile": when this book was first published in 1983, the Waikīkī Movie Theater was slated for demolition.

Waikīkī Theater

However, due to financial constraints of the time, the wrecking ball never made it here! Today it is not only a movie theater, but it also houses IMAX.

This Art Deco movie theater, designed by Charles W. Dickey of Halekūlani fame, was built in 1936. In 1937 it hosted the world premiere of *Waikīkī Wedding*, in which Bing Crosby sang "Sweet Leilani" and "Blue Hawai'i." There are several lovely paintings inside the Kalākaua Avenue lobby as well as the Seaside Avenue (upper) theater lobby.

Victorian lamppost

MIRACLE MILE ✦ **WALK IV**

Waikīkī Theater was known for its unusual interior: a ceiling with moving clouds, and full-scale reproductions of banana and palm trees along the walls. The courtyard was decorated with a fountain and actors' autographs engraved in copper.

Walk around the corner to Seaside Avenue, and when you get to the IMAX look up to view the holes (*puka* in Hawaiian) in the overhang. These *puka* were cut to allow the coconut trees to continue to grow. Only in Hawai'i! Notice the street name at the Seaside entrance of the theater: Lau'ula, meaning 'red leaf.'

Continue along Kalākaua Avenue, crossing easily missed Duke's Lane.

 Duke's Lane

At last sighting, the sign for Duke's Lane was topped with a crown. This street is so narrow that it's easy to miss: just look for a stall-lined lane on the *'Ewa* side.

Duke's Lane is named for Duke Kahanamoku, Hawai'i's most famous

Duke Kahanamoku statue (IX-17)

sportsman and swimmer, who won Olympic medals in 1912, 1920, and 1924 (**II-9**).

Duke Kahanamoku was employed by the Outrigger Canoe Club, which was located across Kalākaua Avenue on the site of the present-day Outrigger Waikīkī Hotel (**IV-15**) until it moved to its present location at the foot of Diamond Head (**VIII-7**). The Outrigger Waikīkī Hotel houses Duke's, a restaurant where Don Ho once sang.

 Macy's Department Store (former *Liberty House*)

Look up! As with the IMAX movie overhang, the overhang of this Macy's department store (formerly *Liberty House*) also has *puka* for its coconut trees. Enjoy the graceful plumeria trees in front of the store.

Federated Department Stores, which own Macy's and Bloomingdale's, took over the Liberty House chain of department stores in 2001. This chain was founded as Hackfeld's Dry Goods in 1849 and renamed H. Hackfeld & Company in 1898; however, in 1918, during World War I, its Germanic name underwent a change to the patriotic-sounding Liberty House (*Liberty* was a buzzword of the day, as in *Liberty Bonds*). Heinrich Hackfeld, a German sea captain who settled in Hawai'i, was one of the founding partners of American Factors, today known as Amfac, Inc., one of Hawai'i's former "Big Five" corporations. The name Hackfeld is preserved as a restaurant in the Ala Moana Shopping Center.

WALK IV ✧ MIRACLE MILE

**International Market Place
(Waikīkī Historic Trail
marker—inside near the
banyan tree)**
 Kaluaokau

The land of the International Market Place, once a summer retreat for Hawaiian royalty, is located on the former 'Āpuakēhau Stream.

Kaluaokau, possibly 'the place of the pit,' was the summer residence of the first elected Hawaiian monarch, King William Charles Lunalilo (1835–1874), who reigned for a little over one year until his death. He left his estate to the wife of King Kamehameha IV, Queen Emma, who also lived here. King Lunalilo founded Lunalilo Home for the Elderly in Hawai'i Kai; Queen Emma, in turn, founded and supported The Queen's Hospital, now The Queen's Medical Center.

International Market Place

The International Market Place, designed by Wimberly and Associates, opened in 1957 with fifty shops, a large number for its time. The Banyan Bazaar, the wooden structure behind the banyan tree, was added in 1978. A structure in the banyan tree, now long gone, was the first home of KCCN Radio, a Hawaiian-music station.

Be sure to check out the Chicken Skin Theater for authentic Hawaiian ghost stories! In the local vernacular, Hawaiian-English Creole, "chicken skin" refers to goose bumps on the skin, as when one is frightened.

 Princess Ka'iulani Shops

In the 1950s the cottage and nursery that were part of the Moana Hotel across the street were razed to make way for the Princess Ka'iulani Shops. The shops, as well as the Princess Ka'iulani Hotel, were designed by architect Gardner Dailey of San Francisco. Dailey also designed a building on the Berkeley campus of the University of California.

Hyatt Regency Waikīkī Hotel
 Peacock Residence

The Walter Peacock home was moved to this site from across the street to make way for the construction of the Moana Hotel wings in 1918.

Eventually the Peacock home was razed and replaced by the *Waikīkī Biltmore*, which, after a twenty-year life, was in turn razed in 1976 to make way for the Hyatt Regency's forty-story twin-tower hotel.

The lobby of the Hyatt Regency is particularly restful, with its massive waterfall, birds, and labeled plants. The upper lobby has lovely display cases, one about *hula* and another filled with Chinese slippers.

Cross Kalākaua Avenue at Uluniu Avenue, just past the Hyatt Regency. Then return toward the beginning of this walk along the *makai* side of Kalākaua.

MIRACLE MILE ✦ **WALK IV**

Moana Hotel (Hawai'i State Archives)

 Police Station
Waikīkī Inn and Tavern
Waikīkī Bowling Alley
Pualeilani

The area between the police station and the main Moana building was land once owned by King Kamehameha IV, who deeded it to a missionary physician, who in turn leased it to various home owners and businesses. Prince Kūhiō's *Pualeilani* summer residence was located near today's surfboard stand.

The *SurfRider Hotel*, now the Diamond Wing of the Sheraton Moana Surfrider Hotel, went up in 1952. Previously, there was a string of homes and small, very popular, businesses, some of which remained until the 1970s. They included the *Waikīkī Tavern*, built in 1884 and later known as the *Waikīkī Inn and Tavern*, with the *Waikīkī Surf Club* housed in the lower level; the all-you-can-eat buffet for seventy-five cents at the *Waikīkī Sands Restaurant*; the *Merry-Go-Round Bar*; *Huddles Restaurant*; *Heine's*, a popular drinking establishment; and *Waikīkī Bowling*. Some of the nonroyal homes between here and "the Wall" (**IX-19**)

were owned by Judge Steiner, Frank Hustace, and Emmanuel S. Cunha.

 Moana Hotel
Sheraton Moana Surfrider Hotel

Sheraton Moana Surfrider Hotel

The original *SurfRider Hotel*, on the Diamond Head side of the Moana, opened in 1952 as Waikīkī's first post-Moana high-rise hotel. Today this eight-story building comprises the Diamond Wing of the Moana Hotel.

In 1969 the present Surfrider Hotel was built 'Ewa of the Moana Hotel, the site of the filled-in streambed of the 'Āpuakēhau Stream. This twenty-one-story building is the Tower Wing.

The colonial-style Moana Hotel (*moana* means 'ocean'), lovingly referred to as the "First Lady of Waikīkī," is

47

WALK IV ÷ MIRACLE MILE

Waikīkī's oldest surviving hotel. It opened on March 11, 1901, to serve the classy "steamboat set" from the U.S. Mainland. This central building is referred to as the Banyan Wing.

The family residence of Walter C. Peacock, an English businessman, was located here in the 1890s. Mr. Peacock invested $150,000 in the building of the Moana Hotel, ensuring that he had an office at the top overlooking the mighty Pacific Ocean. When Hawai'i was still an independent republic, a large new hotel in the middle of Waikīkī was proposed. The idea materialized as the present structure, minus the side wings and two upper floors, which were added in 1918. By that time, Hawai'i had become a United States territory. The hotel building was designed by Minnesota architect Oliver G. Traphagen, who also planned the Archives building in downtown Honolulu, the Castle home (**VIII-8**), and the fire station in Pālama on O'ahu.

The original Moana, designed in an eclectic style of Colonial and Queen Anne, was four stories high and contained seventy-five rooms. The building's interior is of oak and pine, with each floor decorated in a different wood. The first floor is oak; second, mahogany; third floor, maple; fourth floor, *koa*; and fifth, cherry. On the rooftop was an observation tower that housed Walter Peacock's office. The Banyan Wing, the main and central building, is listed on the National Register of Historic Places and boasts the islands' first electric elevator.

The hotel dining room included a dance floor that extended out over the ocean. Alongside the dining room was a 300-foot pier, where locals and tourists walked at night.

On July 3, 1935, the popular "Hawai'i Calls" radio program was first broadcast from the Banyan Court of the Moana Hotel. Webley Edwards and Harry Owens were the originators and producers of the show. Broadcast audiences in the courtyard often numbered two thousand. For years there was a plaque on the almost 100-year-old banyan tree claiming that Robert Louis Stevenson did much of his writing there. However, this tree and Stevenson never met: the tree was planted in 1904 and Stevenson died in Sāmoa in 1894. So much for historical authenticity! This banyan tree, 75 feet tall and 150 feet across, is listed on Hawai'i's Rare and Exceptional Tree list, giving it protection under state law.

Porte-Cochère of Sheraton Moana Surfrider Hotel

In 1959 the Moana was bought by the Sheraton chain, which in turn sold it in 1975 to the Kyo-Ya Company, which also owns the Sheraton Waikīkī Hotel, the Royal Hawaiian Hotel, and the Sheraton Princess Ka'iulani Hotel. In 1987, the hotel began a $50 million renovation, which lasted almost two years. The refurbishment returned many aspects of the hotel to the original 1901 architecture, transporting guests back to its Victorian origins. The beautifully restored hotel reopened in March 1989.

Do spend some time in the Moana's Historical Room, which is replete with video footage of old Waikīkī, photos, artifacts, and facts, on the second floor. Historical tours are offered throughout the week; check on dates and times in the main lobby.

Outrigger Waikīkī Hotel
Outrigger Canoe Club's Original Location
 Duke's Restaurant

On the beach side of this hotel was the original location of the Outrigger Canoe Club, which in 1963 moved to its present location at the foot of Diamond Head.

This present structure, the Outrigger Waikīkī, is graced with lovely taro leaf prints on the exterior of the hotel.

Taro leaf pattern

If you have time, take the escalator to the upper lobby to see an authentic 1880s outrigger canoe, which was restored in 1996. Made of local *koa* wood, it is named *Kaukahi*, 'singleness of purpose.' Also, view the mural of an outrigger canoe on the wall behind the reception desk.

Nearby you'll find a Polynesian star compass table and material that explains ancient voyaging and navigational techniques.

Duke's Restaurant, named for Duke Kahanamoku, Hawai'i's famed sportsman, is the first place in Waikīkī where Don Ho found the spotlight. If you don't have time for a snack or a drink, walk around the restaurant and view the fabulous photos of old.

 Royal Hawaiian Shopping Center

The Royal Hawaiian Shopping Center is a three-block mall with more than 100 shops plus a right-of-way to the beach! The land is owned by Kamehameha Schools, a foundation that administers schools for Hawaiian and part-Hawaiian children. The building material is an aggregate of cement, local volcanic cinder, local coral, and vulcanite. As with King Kalākaua Plaza, these three blocks were formerly filled with smaller stores. When the Royal Hawaiian Shopping Center was first built, the locals called it Fort Bishop due to its austere façade and its ownership by the Bishop Estate.

The Royal Hawaiian Shopping Center offers much more than conventional shopping. Activities are also offered here, including *lei* making,

WALK IV ❖ MIRACLE MILE

hula lessons, and torch lighting—every night a torch lighter sets the fifty torches aflame. As you meander around, notice all the Hawaiian elements in this shopping center: the flowers, lava walls, and torches. A pathway out the back leads to the Royal Hawaiian Hotel (**IX-9**).

The pool and sculpture of Hawaiian torch fisherman by C. W. Watson were installed in 1980.

This is also a good vantage point from which to view the beautiful tapa design on the Macy's building across the street. Tapa is a local fabric made from native plants. Designs similar to the one on the building across the way are placed on the fabric. In the coffee tables of the Tapa Tower of the Hilton Hawaiian Village (**II-12**), there is an excellent display and explanation of tapa making.

At the corner is the Waikīkī Trolley information booth.

After the three blocks of the Royal Hawaiian Shopping Center is Lewers Street. Cross Lewers to the bank on the corner.

First Hawaiian Bank
Jean Charlot Fresco Murals

First Hawaiian Bank, founded in 1858, is the oldest financial institution in Hawai'i, with sixty branches in Hawai'i and the Pacific. It is a subsidiary of BancWest corporation, a regional financial services corporation; BancWest is a subsidiary of BNP Paribas, France's largest publicly traded bank.

The bank branch on the *makai-'Ewa* corner of Kalākaua Avenue and Lewers Street is famous for its huge frescoes. If you are here during banking hours, go in to appreciate these fine murals up close; otherwise, peering in will have to suffice!

The murals were created by artist Jean Charlot. Coincidentally, given that the bank is now French owned, Charlot was born in Paris. He lived in Mexico from 1920 to 1929, where he studied under Diego Rivera, spent the following twenty years at various universities in the United States, and arrived in Hawai'i in 1949, where he remained, enamored of its culture, until his death thirty years later.

These paneled murals, *Early Contacts of Hawai'i with Outer World*, painted in 1966, portray the lives of Hawaiians through the years from before Captain Cook's arrival to the time of the missionaries.

The series begins on the *mauka* wall:

- On the left, the Hawaiians of old making *kapa*, or bark cloth.
- On the right, a high chief and his wife returning from a visit to Captain Cook's ships. An image of a Hawaiian god is held by a *kahuna*, a professional specialist—in this instance, in religion.

The series continues on the *makai* wall, above the tellers' booths, from left to right:

- The 1820s, when the missionaries introduced the *mu'umu'u*, which was patterned after the slip worn by the missionary women beneath their heavy dresses.
- Kamehameha I posing for his only known portrait, by Louis Choris, the artist with the Russian expedition of 1816–17 under Captain von Kotzebue (next scene).

- Kamehameha I receiving Otto von Kotzebue, leader of a Russian expedition. Von Kotzebue is standing with his back to us.
- The sandalwood trade, represented by two men facing us: Boki, a Hawaiian *ali'i*, or royalty, and a Chinese merchant, perhaps Chun Afong, "merchant prince of the sandalwood mountains" (**II-6**), holding a native sandalwood branch. Because of the many sandalwood trees and the Chinese love for it, Hawai'i was referred to as the "sandalwood mountains."
- Beginnings of contact and trade in 1778, as represented by kegs and animals. The Hawaiians traded their capes and helmets for kegs of nails and metal tools, and their pigs for imported goats, cattle, and horses.
- The first printing press introduced into the islands in 1822. Kamehameha II is standing in uniform behind the press. Missionary Elisha Loomis worked prodigiously with books and printing.
- Missionary woman teaching the alphabet to Hawaiian children.
- The uncarved lava stone is an *akua*, 'image of a god,' representing the lost Hawaiian religion. The solitary Hawaiian represents the lost art of the *kāhuna*, the educated professional class (Kāhuna Stones **IX-15**).

You can find other Charlot frescoes at the University of Hawai'i at Mānoa in Bachman Hall and in Jefferson Hall, as well as in the Jean Charlot Collection at Hamilton Library. A ceramic-tiled statue of an *ali'i*, a Hawaiian chief, by Charlot stands at the *makai* corner of the Ala Moana Hotel on Atkinson Drive, Diamond Head of the Ala Moana Shopping Center.

Walk *makai* along Lewers Street to Helumoa Road.

 Ohana Edgewater Hotel

Go inside the *makai* 'oceanside' lobby of the Ohana Edgewater Hotel to view the photos of old Waikīkī and Hawai'i from the Hawai'i State Archives: an 1873 photo of old Waikīkī; photos of celebrities of years past, including Eddie Cantor, Shirley Temple, and Groucho Marx; and a January 19, 1948, menu from the SS *Matsonia*, which docked at Honolulu Harbor.

This is the end of **Walk IV**. You are about two blocks Diamond Head and two blocks *makai* from the beginning of this walk.

If you wish to continue walking:
- Walk one block 'Ewa to Beach Walk to **Walk III**, which begins on Helumoa Road and Beach Walk (one block 'Ewa of Lewers Street), to learn about the Hawaiian monarchs who once lived on the beaches of Waikīkī; or
- Take **Walk II**, which begins a few blocks 'Ewa and *makai* at the entrance to the Hilton Hawaiian Village, at the intersection of Ala Moana Boulevard and Kālia Road, to follow in the footsteps of the early Hawaiians in this area.

Prince Kawananakoa, Eva Parker (of the Big Island Parker ranch family), Rose Cleghorn and Princess Ka'iulani, 1898 (Hawai'i State Archives)

Walk V
· Last Days of the Monarchy ·

Princess Ka'iulani statue

Walk V
Last Days of the Monarchy
Central Waikīkī

🕐 **TIME:** 1.5 hours

➪ **DISTANCE:** 1.5 miles (2.4 kilometers)

O N JANUARY 17, 1893, AFTER A TWO-YEAR REIGN, QUEEN LILI'UOKALANI WAS OVERTHROWN BY FOREIGN BUSINESSMEN, SOME OF WHOM WERE SONS OF THE MISSIONARIES WHO HAD MADE HAWAI'I THEIR HOME. ON THAT DATE THE HAWAIIAN MONARCHY OFFICIALLY ENDED. This walk focuses on the lives of Hawai'i's last two monarchs, King Kalākaua and Queen Lili'uokalani, and their relatives, at the end of the nineteenth century. The royal personages mentioned here are:

King Kalākaua
Lived: 1836–1891
Ruled: 1874–1891
Spouse: Queen Kapi'olani

Queen Lili'uokalani
Lived: 1838–1917
Ruled: 1891–1893
Spouse: Gov. John Owen Dominis Holt

Princess Likelike
Lived: 1851–1887
Spouse: Gov. Archibald Scott Cleghorn

Princess Ka'iulani
Lived: 1875–1899
(never married)

King Kalākaua, Queen Lili'uokalani, and Princess Likelike were siblings; Princess Ka'iulani was the daughter of Princess Likelike.

The Kalākaua lineage was related to Kamehameha I through a common ancestor. When the Kamehameha line failed to produce an heir to the throne, Lunalilo, grandson of a half brother to Kamehameha I, was appointed king by the Hawai'i legislature. When he died a year later, the legislature elected David La'amea Kalākaua as king in 1874. His sister, Lili'uokalani, ascended to the throne in 1891 on Kalākaua's death in San Francisco.

This walk passes through the areas of two royal residences: 'Āinahau and Hamohamo. The only reminder of 'Āinahau is 'Āinahau Park (**V-5**). Nothing remains of Hamohamo—even Hamohamo Street, which once ran between Kāneloa Road and Cartwright Road, no longer exists. ⚜

➤ **BEGIN WALK:** *This walk starts at the Sheraton Princess Ka'iulani Hotel on Ka'iulani Avenue, across from King's Village, and meanders along several streets in this area.*

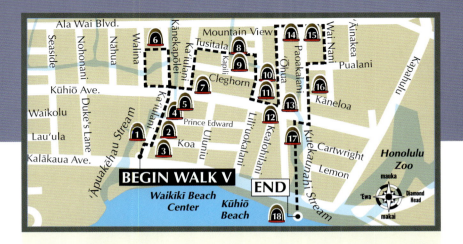

WALK V

Last Days of the Monarchy

Central Waikīkī

NINE WALKS THROUGH TIME

- **V-1** Sheraton Princess Ka'iulani Hotel
  'Āinahau
  'Au'aukai
- **V-2** King's Village Shopping Center
  Uluniu
- **V-3** Koa Avenue
- **V-4** Prince Edward Street
- **V-5** Princess Ka'iulani Park
  'Āinahau Park
- **V-6** Kānekapōlei Street Banyan Tree
- **V-7** Cleghorn Street
- **V-8** Tusitala Street
  The Jungle
- **V-9** Kapili Street
- **V-10** Lili'uokalani Avenue
  Hamohamo
- **V-11** Radisson Waikīkī Prince Kūhiō Hotel
- **V-12** Kealohilani Avenue
- **V-13** 'Ōhua Avenue
- **V-14** Paoakalani Street
- **V-15** Wai Nani Way
  Paoakalani
- **V-16** Kāneloa Road
  Kāneloa
  Kekio
- **V-17** Waikīkī Beach Marriott Hotel
- **V-18** Kūhiō Beach Park
  Pualeilani
  Uluniu

※ 55 ※

WALK V ✣ LAST DAYS OF THE MONARCHY

Sheraton Princess Ka'iulani Hotel
'Āinahau
'Au'aukai

The ancient Hawaiians called this section of Waikīkī *Au'aukai*, meaning 'to bathe in the sea.' In more recent times, it was known as *'Āinahau*. This was the area in Waikīkī that Princess Victoria Kawēkiu I Lunalilo Kalaninuiahilapalapa Ka'iulani Cleghorn (or Princess Ka'iulani, as she is popularly known) called home. Ka'iulani means 'the royal sacred heights.'

Around the end of the nineteenth century, when the Cleghorns (Princess Ka'iulani's family) lived here, they called their land *'Āinahau*, meaning 'land of the *hau* tree.' The *hau* tree is related to the hibiscus plant and was common here until *'Āpuakēhau Stream* (**I-9**) was diverted from Waikīkī during the building of the Ala Wai Canal. Today few *hau* trees are found here, but they abound along the Ala Wai Canal and on the beaches. *'Āpuakēhau Stream* flowed through the land, *mauka* and *'Ewa*. It is said that Princess Ka'iulani traveled downstream in a small boat to the ocean!

'Āinahau had plentiful flora and fauna—especially peacocks, Ka'iulani's favorite bird.

A ten-acre plot of land was given to the princess as a christening gift on December 25, 1875, by her aunt, Princess Ruth Ke'elikōlani. Princess Ruth (1826–1883) had inherited the land from her father, who was a governor of O'ahu and husband of Kamehameha I's daughter, Pauahi. Princess Ka'iulani called her aunt Mama Nui, 'Big Mama'! Princess Likelike, Princess Ka'iulani's mother, died at *'Āinahau* in 1887 at the age of thirty-six, when Ka'iulani was only twelve.

Princess Ka'iulani
(Hawai'i State Archives)

Princess Ka'iulani spent eight years as a student in England. In 1897, while she was away at school, her father, O'ahu Governor Archibald Cleghorn, built a two-story Victorian house with a tower. It was located approximately two blocks Diamond Head and *mauka* of the present-day Princess Ka'iulani Hotel. The architect was Clinton Briggs Ripley.

Poet and author Robert Louis Stevenson (**V-8**) was a close friend of Ka'iulani's family, and he often read to the princess during his stays in Hawai'i. It is said that these readings took place beneath one of the many banyan trees, perhaps one similar to the huge tree near Kānekapōlei Street (**V-6**). The banyan tree at *'Āinahau* was cut down due to decay, but a cutting was taken and planted at the Princess Ka'iulani Elementary School in Honolulu, where it still stands. The banyan, a ficus, can reach 100 feet in height. It is supported by its aerial

'Āinahau *(Hawai'i State Archives)*

roots, which hang down and become embedded in the soil, thereby serving as secondary trunks.

Princess Ka'iulani died at *'Āinahau* in 1899 soon after returning from Washington, D.C., where she met with President McKinley in the hope of restoring the monarchy. Following the trip to America, she went to the Big Island and fell ill while riding a horse in the rain. She died shortly after, on March 6, at the age of twenty-three.

In 1910, Princess Ka'iulani's father also died at *'Āinahau*. Since he had no heirs, he willed the family lands to the Hawaiian government with the hope that *'Āinahau* would be used to augment Kapi'olani Park (**VII-1**). The government accepted the land, but with the overthrow of the Hawaiian monarchy, the area was subdivided, depriving Kapi'olani Park of this lovely addition. Only the *'Āinahau* peacock flock became part of the park; the peacocks in the Honolulu Zoo may well be descendants of Ka'iulani's favorite birds. The elegant home that

Archibald Cleghorn had lovingly built was destroyed by fire in the 1920s.

Upon subdivision of the *'Āinahau* land, the grass-thatched houses on the property were to be destroyed. Fortunately, Rachel Payne of the Salvation Army noticed a newspaper ad offering the grass houses located on the property for sale. One of them was purchased by James Bergstrom, who donated it to the Salvation Army and had it moved to the Wai'oli 'joyful water' Tea Room grounds in Mānoa Valley (**I-3**), where it stands to this day. Although it has not been documented, that grass shack is said to be the "little grass shack" where Stevenson lived, wrote, and worked, and perhaps even read to Princess Ka'iulani. At the very least, an authentic grass shack has been preserved! The interior posts of the hut are made of *'ōhi'a* wood, an endemic (found only in Hawai'i and nowhere else) tree. The thatch was originally of native *pili* grasses but has been replaced by the more available exotic (non-native) broom grass.

WALK V ⁂ LAST DAYS OF THE MONARCHY

The Princess Ka'iulani Hotel, one of Waikīkī's earliest high-rises, was constructed in 1954 by Matson Navigation, a local transportation company established in 1880. It officially opened on Kamehameha Day, June 11, in 1955. Matson had also built several other hotels: the Moana, the Royal Hawaiian, and the original *SurfRider*. Today all these hotels are part of the Sheraton chain. The entryway of the Princess Ka'iulani Hotel is particularly attractive, with waterfalls flowing over lava, and graceful koi (a type of goldfish) swimming in the pool below.

The architect for the Princess Ka'iulani Hotel was Gardner Dailey, who also designed the Princess Ka'iulani Shops (**IV-11**) on Kalākaua Avenue. In the lobby is a striking portrait of the princess, with a *koa* wood case displaying photographs and objects connected with her life. The lobby is filled with photographs of the princess and her family in 'Āinahau, and local artisans set up their wearable works of art for display and sale.

Plumeria

The plants surrounding the pool are particularly attractive: plumeria trees (with a popular flower for *lei*); ficus (fig) trees with large, round leaves; coconut palm trees; and money plants (*Dracaena*) with long, pointed leaves—all exotics or non-native plants that grow beautifully in the Hawaiian climate. The lava stone bench, which was in front of the banyan tree at 'Āinahau, is now in the *mauka-'Ewa* area of the pool, near the restaurant. A bronze plaque points out the bench and ceremonial stone.

Cross Ka'iulani Avenue to King's Village Shopping Center across the way.

King's Village Shopping Center (Waikīkī Historic Trail marker)
2 *Uluniu*

King's Village Shopping Center

In the 1800s, *Uluniu*, 'coconut grove,' referred to a grove of thousands of coconut trees that surrounded the royal residences from this area down to the ocean. Uluniu Avenue, one block Diamond Head of King's Village, is a reminder of the former "King's Coconut Grove" (**III-9**).

King's Village Shopping Center,

formerly King's Alley, directly across from the Sheraton Princess Ka'iulani Hotel, was built in 1972 in a retro style to re-create the British flavor King Kalākaua had admired so much during his trip around the world in the 1880s. King Kalākaua was particularly attracted to the style of the Victorian British Empire. The King's Village guards are especially picturesque, with uniforms said to be reproductions of those worn by the Hawaiian Royal Palace guards during Kalākaua's reign, 1874–1891. At 6:00 P.M. daily, a 1919 London bell chimes. This is the very bell that rang in England at the inception of the Allied invasion in Europe. The chiming of the bell is followed by the changing of the king's guard ceremony at King's Village at 6:15 P.M., under the banyan tree on the corner of Koa and Ka'iulani avenues.

King's Village courtyard

Go into the courtyard for a surprise. In the Variety Club Celebrity Circle are the handprints of some famous people, including Sammy Davis Jr., Don Ho, and Robert Cazimero (a local Hawaiian singer).

Notice the names of the streets meeting Ka'iulani Avenue on either side of King's Village. The two streets are named for Prince Kūhiō's (**V-18**) brothers. The three brothers were adopted by King Kalākaua and Queen Kapi'olani, who had no children of their own.

 Koa Avenue (*makai* of King's Village)

Koa, a native Hawaiian hardwood, means 'brave' or 'soldier' and refers here to Prince David Kawānanakoa, a brother of Prince Kūhiō, who lived near here from 1868 to 1908. Prince Kawānanakoa, 'brave or fearless prophecy,' was named for a battle in Nu'uanu, a valley *mauka* of downtown Honolulu.

 Prince Edward Street (*mauka* of King's Village)

This street is named for Prince Edward Keli'iahonui, another brother of Prince Kūhiō, who lived here from 1869 to 1887. Keli'iahonui means 'the long suffering, patient chief.'

Walk *mauka* to the grassy park.

 Princess Ka'iulani Park (Waikīkī Historic Trail marker) 'Āinahau Park

'*Āinahau*, 'land of the *hau* tree,' as this entire district was known 100 years ago, survives today as the name of this small grassy area. This park likely would have been the beginning of the palm-lined driveway into the 'Āinahau manor, which stood *mauka* of this point.

This lovely statue of Princess Ka'iulani, draped with *lei* made from her favorite flower, Chinese jasmine (*pīkake* in

WALK V ✣ LAST DAYS OF THE MONARCHY

'Āinahau driveway (Hawai'i State Archives)

Hawaiian), was dedicated on the 124th anniversary of her birth, October 16,1999. Notice the peacock (her favorite bird), also *pīkake* in Hawaiian, at her feet. The inscription reveals her royal lineage and various aspects of her life. The statue was commissioned by the Kelley family, owners of the Outrigger Hotel chain, and was created by Jan Gordon Fisher, who also fashioned the statue of Duke Kahanamoku at Kūhiō Beach (**IX-17**). Princess Ka'iulani's statue is surrounded by hibiscus plants, red ti plants, papaya trees, and twenty-three coconut trees, one for each year of her life. Notice her full Hawaiian name on the plaque.

Cross Kūhiō Avenue at Kānekapōlei Street and walk *'Ewa* to Walina 'softness' Street, then walk *mauka* halfway up Walina, to a large parking area. Walk through the parking lot—in the middle is one of the largest banyan trees in Waikīkī. Continue through to Kānekapōlei Street.

 Kānekapōlei Street Banyan Tree

Although this banyan tree is not on *'Āinahau* property, it is the type of tree around which legends of Robert Lewis Stevenson and Princess Ka'iulani flourished. In 1978 the property owners proposed removing the old tree in order to enlarge the parking lot. Fortunately, public and private opposition was so great that the tree was only trimmed back.

Banyan tree

Kānekapōlei is named for Marion Kānekapōlei Guerrero Diamond, a resident of this area in the 1930s, who was named for the uncle of a wife of King Kamehameha I. Kānekapōlei is also the name of a god of flowers.

Walk back to Kūhiō Avenue and continue Diamond Head. Then turn *mauka* onto Ka'iulani Avenue, passing Cleghorn Street.

 Cleghorn Street

Archibald Scott Cleghorn was born in Scotland, and in 1851, at the age of sixteen, he immigrated to Hawai'i with his parents. In Honolulu, Cleghorn met and married Princess Kapili Likelike in 1870, who bore their only child, Princess Ka'iulani, five years later.

Cleghorn was named governor of O'ahu in 1891, after the death of John Dominis, husband of Queen Lili'uokalani and governor of Hawai'i.

He was the first president of The Queen's Hospital, a major medical facility in Hawai'i, known today as The Queen's Medical Center. Cleghorn also owned an import and dry goods store on Nu'uanu Street in downtown Honolulu.

Archibald Scott Cleghorn (Hawai'i State Archives)

As the first commissioner of parks, he is remembered as the father of Honolulu's park system. As vice president of the Kapi'olani Park Association in the 1870s, he was instrumental in designing this particular park (**Walk VII**), especially the trees. Always interested in plants, Cleghorn also developed a beautiful garden around his home in '*Āinahau*.

Continue *mauka* on Ka'iulani Avenue until you reach Tusitala Street. Walk Diamond Head on Tusitala Street all the way through on the path to Lili'uokalani Avenue. The vegetation is lovely here: coconut trees, ti plants, and even taro plants, reminiscent of the taro ponds of old (**Walk II**).

 **Tusitala Street
The Jungle**

Mauka of this street is the site of the Cleghorn home. The entire area, all around, was '*Āinahau*.

Tusitala Street garden

"Tusitala" was Robert Louis Stevenson's Samoan name, meaning 'teller of tales.' (Samoan and Hawaiian are related languages, both belonging to the Polynesian family.)

Stevenson stayed in Hawai'i for five months in 1889 and made a shorter visit again in 1893, staying at Sans Souci Beach (**VIII-5** and **6**). Stevenson, who was born in Scotland, became a close friend of his compatriot, Governor Cleghorn. He often read to Cleghorn's daughter, Princess Ka'iulani, and he wrote to her during his second visit to Hawai'i, while she was away, studying in England. Stevenson continued on to Sāmoa, where he died.

House on Tusitala Street

WALK V ✦ LAST DAYS OF THE MONARCHY

Until recently this area was called "the jungle" because it was thick as a jungle with small wooden houses and small apartment complexes. Although high-rise condominiums and hotels have encroached on "the jungle," it still contains many interesting small-frame houses. Walk leisurely along this street, appreciating the intimacy of the neighborhood and visualizing ʻĀinahau.

Continue on Tusitala on the stone path. Notice the vegetation: betel nut tree, and red and green ti plants.

Kapili Street

Kapili Street connects Tusitala and Cleghorn streets at the Diamond Head end. It is named for Princess Miriam Kapili Likelike (1851–1887), sister of King Kalākaua and Queen Liliʻuokalani, and mother of Princess Kaʻiulani. Likelike Highway, which connects this side of Oʻahu with the windward side of the island, is also named for her.

Walk *makai* on Liliʻuokalani Avenue to Kūhiō Avenue.

Liliʻuokalani Avenue
Hamohamo

This street is named for Queen Lydia Liliʻuokalani, who lived from 1838 to 1917, and reigned from 1891 to 1893 (**I-8**). One of Queen Liliʻuokalani's houses, *Paoakalani*, was located *mauka* of this area, between Paoakalani Street and Wai Nani Way. She owned a large tract of land extending from today's Ala Wai Canal to the beach between Liliʻuokalani Avenue and Wai Nani Way, connecting with a 1,400-foot strip of beachfront land (today's Kūhiō Beach), the location of her second home, *Kealohilani*.

Queen Liliʻuokalani
(Hawaiʻi State Archives)

During royal times the queen's land was known as *Hamohamo*, meaning 'rub gently' (**III-7**), referring perhaps to the action of the water on the sand. *Kuekaunahi Stream* ran through *Hamohamo* from the Koʻolau Mountains, to near Kapahulu Avenue, Diamond Head of here, and out to the Pacific Ocean at "the Wall" (**IX-19**). The stream was diverted to the Ala Wai Canal in the 1920s.

Walk *makai* along Liliʻuokalani Avenue, then Diamond Head on Kūhiō Avenue. As you continue around the corner of the Prince Kūhiō Hotel, notice the stately fan palm trees.

Radisson Waikīkī Prince Kūhiō Hotel

Stop in at the Prince Kūhiō Hotel to view Hawaiian artifacts and the photos of Prince Kūhiō in the display cases. A statue of Prince Kūhiō is located at Kūhiō Beach (**IX-16**) between ʻŌhua and Liliʻuokalani avenues.

Continue Diamond Head on Kūhiō Avenue, turning *mauka* on 'Ōhua Avenue. You will pass Kealohilani Avenue on the other side of Kūhiō.

 Kealohilani Avenue

Kealohilani, which connects Kūhiō and Kalākaua avenues on the *makai* side, is a traditional Hawaiian name from early times meaning 'the royal brightness' or 'the glitter of heaven.' This street was named for Queen Lili'uokalani's residence at Kūhiō Beach, which she referred to as her "pretty seaside cottage." However, the name had been used earlier by Kamehameha V for his beach home at *Helumoa* as well (**III-3**).

Kealohilani was also the name of members of the royal family and the name of a star that rises in the night of *Mauli*, during the month of *Welo* (corresponding to March or April), and sets in the night of *Muku* in the month of *Māhoe Mua* (most likely a summer month). A ring around this star is said to portend revolution, and indeed a ring did appear around the star Kealohilani shortly before the overthrow of the monarchy in 1893.

Walk *mauka* on 'Ōhua Avenue past the

Waikīkī Banyan Hotel

Waikīkī Banyan Hotel. Notice the banyan trees at both ends of the hotel, one on Kūhiō, the other just past it on 'Ōhua.

 'Ōhua Avenue

'Ōhua means 'retainer' or 'servant,' and refers to the retainers of King Kalākaua and of Queen Lili'uokalani, who were housed along this street.

Continue along 'Ōhua to the Ala Wai Canal, then walk Diamond Head past Paoakalani Street, and then walk *makai* on Wai Nani 'beautiful water' Way.

 Paoakalani Street

Paoakalani, the name of Queen Lili'uokalani's principal home (next stop), means the 'royal perfume.' As you pass this street, look back on the *'Ewa* side to see cutout crosses on the side of a small building. This was once the elementary school and convent connected with St. Augustine Church (**VI-1** and **6**).

On the *makai* side of Ala Wai Boulevard are lovely plantings of green and red ti leaves.

Turn *makai* on Wai Nani Way to the entrance to Lili'uokalani Gardens.

 Wai Nani Way
Paoakalani

Queen Lili'uokalani's primary home, *Paoakalani*, was located where the Lili'uokalani Garden Towers are today. Built in 1983, this complex, King Tower on the *mauka* side and Queen Tower on the *makai* side, replaced small homes similar to those

WALK V ✦ LAST DAYS OF THE MONARCHY

on the surrounding street. The queen's home was most likely located at the King Tower—yes, it should have been Queen Tower! Walk into the driveway area to admire the lovely gardens and ponds. Notice the interesting crest of flowers in the center of the driveway.

Enjoy walking *makai* in the cool shade of the banyan trees along Wai Nani, then walk ʻEwa on Pualani Way, which means 'flower of heaven' and may refer, figuratively, to the royalty who once lived here. Return to Paoakalani Street, walking *makai* past Kāneloa Road to the Waikīkī Beach Marriott Hotel.

Kāneloa Road
Kāneloa
Kekio

Kāneloa means 'long or tall man,' but Kāne is also the name of an important Hawaiian god. Kāneloa Road is named for a tract of land that extended from this area through Kapiʻolani Park between the Ala Wai Canal and Kūhiō Avenue.

The area directly *makai* of *Kāneloa* was known as *Kekio*, 'the protuberance.'

Continue *makai* on Paoakalani, crossing Kūhiō Avenue to the Waikīkī Beach Marriott Hotel.

Waikīkī Beach Marriott Hotel

This hotel is located near the former *Kuekaunahi Stream* that flowed through Waikīkī before the 1920s. Opened in 1972, it was originally named the Hawaiian Regent. The two towers are named after Queen Liliʻuokalani's homes: Kealohilani, the first tower, and Paoakalani, built in 1979.

Walk through the hotel and exit onto Kalākaua Avenue at Kūhiō Beach Park.

Kūhiō Beach Park
Pualeilani
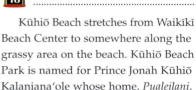
Uluniu

Kūhiō Beach stretches from Waikīkī Beach Center to somewhere along the grassy area on the beach. Kūhiō Beach Park is named for Prince Jonah Kūhiō Kalanianaʻole whose home, *Pualeilani*, was nearby. A statue of Prince Kūhiō is located at Kūhiō Beach between ʻŌhua and Liliʻuokalani avenues.

Prince Kūhiō served as a delegate to the United States Congress from 1902 until his death in 1922. He was instrumental in enacting the Hawaiian Homes Commission Act, which granted two hundred thousand acres of land to native Hawaiians.

Kūhiō's death marked the end of an era: the royal realm at Waikīkī would be no longer. This beach was dedicated to him in 1940. Kūhiō Day, a state holiday, is celebrated on March 26.

When Kūhiō's mother died shortly after his birth in 1871, he and his brothers

Prince Jonah Kūhiō and wife horseback riding in the country (Hawaiʻi State Archives)

(**V-2** to **4**) were adopted by their aunt, Kalākaua's wife. When Kalākaua became king in 1874, he gave royal titles to his sisters, Lili'uokalani (**V-10**) and Miriam Likelike, and to his foster child, Kūhiō. Queen Lili'uokalani later gave a portion of her *Hamohamo* estate to Kūhiō.

Since King Kalākaua and Queen Kapi'olani owned a summer home here, it was probably they who gave the property its name, *Pualeilani*, meaning 'flower from the wreath of heaven.' The name *Pualeilani* was also used by Queen Lili'uokalani as one of her homes.

- **Walk VII**, Kapi'olani Park and Honolulu Zoo, *makai* from here at the intersection of Monsarrat and Kalākaua avenues.

Coconut trees along the beach

Uluniu, 'coconut grove,' referred to a grove of several thousand coconut trees that surrounded King Kalākaua's residence here. The coconut trees along the beach today are descendants of trees that were here at the time of the early Hawaiian monarchs.

Uluniu Avenue is *mauka*-Diamond Head, named in honor of the royalty who once lived here.

This is the conclusion of **Walk V**. If you wish to continue walking, take:
- **Walk VI**, Local Life in Waikīkī Today. Start at St. Augustine Church on Kalākaua and 'Ōhua avenues; or

Vendor and shopper at the People's Open Market (VI-15)

Walk VI
· Local Life Today in Waikīkī ·

Walk VI
Local Life Today in Waikīkī
Mauka-Diamond Head end of Waikīkī: from the Ala Wai Canal to Kapahulu Avenue

🕐 **TIME:** 1.5 hours
➩ **DISTANCE:** 1.25 miles (2 kilometers)

Date palms

THIS WALK INTRODUCES A NUMBER OF PUBLIC SERVICE INSTITUTIONS SERVING WAIKĪKĪ RESIDENTS AND VISITORS: CHURCHES, THE COMMUNITY CENTER, LIBRARIES, SCHOOLS, GARDENS, THE MARKET, THE FIRE STATION, AND THE PARK.

The tour covers a portion of the land areas, or *'ili*, once known as *Kāneloa* and *Kekio*. *Kāneloa*, the larger of the two, extended into Kapi'olani Park; *Kekio* was located *makai* of *Kāneloa* (**VI-5**). ❦

▶ **BEGIN WALK:** *Start at St. Augustine Church on Kalākaua and 'Ōhua avenues.*

As you walk **mauka**, *away from the hustle and bustle of Waikīkī, you will enter the world of the lives of people who work in, and perhaps were born and continue to live in, Waikīkī.*

 St. Augustine Church

The original St. Augustine-by-the-Sea Church was established in 1854 for local Catholics. In the summer of 1898, during the Spanish-American War, the soldiers who camped at nearby Kapi'olani Park (**VII-1**) were among its congregants. That first Hawaiian-style, open-latticework church was built by

St. Augustine Church

the priest himself. By the early 1960s the building had been so seriously termite damaged that it was replaced by the present French/Gothic-style church, designed by local architect George McLaughlin.

The interior is highlighted by stained-glass windows made in Innsbruck, Austria, by *Tiroler Glasmalerei und Mosaik Anstalt* (Tiroler Glass Painting and Mosaic Institute). The baptismal font, dating to the time of the monarchy, was presented to the church by Prince David and Princess

WALK VI
Local Life Today in Waikīkī

Mauka-Diamond Head end of Waikīkī from the Ala Wai Canal to Kapahulu Avenue

NINE WALKS THROUGH TIME

VI-1   St. Augustine Church
VI-2   Damien Museum
VI-3   Lemon Road
VI-4   Cartwright Road
VI-5   Kāneloa Road
       Kāneloa
       Kekio
VI-6   Waikīkī Community
       Center Complex
       Paoakalani Street
VI-7   Jefferson Elementary
       School
       Jefferson School
       Orthopedic Unit
VI-8   Thurston Circle
       Kapahulu Avenue
VI-9   Waikīkī-Kapahulu Public
       Library

VI-10 Waikīkī Fire Station:
       Station No. 7
VI-11 Pākī Avenue, Pākī Park,
       and Pākī Playground
VI-12 Queen Kapiʻolani
       Hibiscus Garden
VI-13 Monsarrat Avenue
VI-14 Waikīkī School
VI-15 People's Open Market—
       If It's Wednesday
       Morning, You're in
       Luck!
VI-16 Diamond Head
       Community Gardens
VI-17 Pākī Hale
       3840 Pākī Avenue
VI-18 Kapiʻolani Park

Abigail Kawānanakoa on the baptism of their daughter, Kapiʻolani, who lived from 1834 (or 1836—the date is in dispute) to 1899 (**VII-1**).

St. Augustine-by-the-Sea is so named because it was once visible from ships at sea. Today it is partially obstructed by the building fronting it on Kalākaua Avenue. However, its copper roof is quite striking when viewed from the ocean or air.

Its elementary school was located *mauka* of here, on Paoakalani Street. Today that building houses the Waikīkī Community Center (**VI-6**).

 Damien Museum

Damien Museum

The Damien Museum is located in a small building behind and *ʻEwa* of St. Augustine Church. It commemorates the life and humanitarian works of Father Damien (Joseph de Veuster, 1840–1889), a Belgian priest who dedicated his life to those with Hansen's disease (leprosy) at the Kalaupapa settlement on the island of Molokaʻi. After sixteen years of ministering to the people of Kalaupapa, he, himself, died of leprosy. Admission to the museum is free, but donations are appreciated. The museum is open weekdays from 9:00 A.M. to 3:00 P.M.

*Father Damien
(Joseph de Veuster, 1840–1889)
(Hawaiʻi State Archives)*

A stylized bronze statue of Father Damien stands in front of the Hawaiʻi State Capitol on King Street. This statue is a copy of one by Marisol Escobar. The original is one of two Hawaiʻi statues in the U.S. Capitol in Washington, D.C.; the other statue is of King Kamehameha I.

Walk back to Kalākaua Avenue, turn Diamond Head to Paoakalani Avenue, continue *mauka*, crossing Lemon and Cartwright roads, both named for foreigners who settled in Hawaiʻi and contributed to its development.

 Lemon Road

James Silas Lemon, a Frenchman who lived in Hawaiʻi from 1849 to 1882, was a land developer in nearby Kaimukī (**I-4**).

 Cartwright Road

This road is named for either Alexander Joy Cartwright Jr., who came to Hawaiʻi in 1849 and whose home predated Fort DeRussy (**II-6**), or his son, Bruce, one of the subdividers of Waikīkī. The elder Cartwright is referred to as the "father of modern baseball"—he was one of the main authors of the game's rules and regulations.

After you cross Kūhiō Avenue and pass Kāneloa Road on the Diamond Head side, continue to 310 Paoakalani Avenue on the 'Ewa side of the street.

Kāneloa Road
Kāneloa
5 Kekio

Kāneloa Road is named for a tract of land that extended from this area up through Kapi'olani Park between the Ala Wai Canal and Kūhiō Avenue. *Kāneloa* means 'long or tall man,' but Kāne is also the name of a very important Hawaiian god.

The area directly *makai* of *Kāneloa* was known as *Kekio*, 'the protuberance.'

Waikīkī Community Center Complex
6 Paoakalani Street

Paoakalani, 'royal perfume,' was the name of Queen Lili'uokalani's principal home in Waikīkī (**V-14** and **15**).

The Waikīkī Community Center, which extends from 310 Paoakalani Street through to 277 'Ōhua Avenue, houses various community groups such as clinics, a preschool, a senior center, and church organizations. From 1929 to 1980, St. Augustine Church's convent and school were located here, hence the crosses on the Paoakalani side of the center.

A farmers' market has the place jumping on Tuesday and Thursday mornings.

Double back on Paoakalani Street, then walk Diamond Head on Pualani Way, which means 'flower of heaven' and may refer, figuratively, to the royalty who once lived here. (Refer to **Walk V**, Last Days of the Monarchy)

Pualani Way veers *mauka* to become 'Āinakea 'white land' Way. Straight ahead are several school buildings.

Jefferson Elementary School
Jefferson School
7 Orthopedic Unit

The two Jefferson schools, named after President Thomas Jefferson, date to 1931. The original school structure burned to the ground in 1980. Jefferson Elementary is kindergarten through grade six; Jefferson Orthopedic, in the *makai* building, is a K–12 program for children with severe disabilities.

The enrollment at Jefferson has diminished as more and more family dwellings in the area have been displaced by hotels and condominiums. However, over the past few years, it has been stable at about five hundred children.

On the school grounds is a lovely marble sculpture, *E Pluribus Unum*, by local artist Eli Marozzi. In Marozzi's words, this sculpture of intertwined faces and arms symbolizes that "we are many, but we can attain oneness in harmony."

The colorful hand-painted ceramic tiles all around the school have been created by students, staff, parents, and the local community.

Continue up to the canal, then walk Diamond Head to the grassy area and fountain at the intersection of Ala Wai Boulevard and Kapahulu Avenue.

WALK VI ✥ LOCAL LIFE TODAY IN WAIKĪKĪ

 Thurston Circle
8 Kapahulu Avenue

The park-like triangle at this intersection is known as Thurston Circle, named for Lorrin Andrews Thurston (1858–1931), the son of early missionaries. Thurston was a lawyer, newspaper publisher (*The Honolulu Advertiser*), one of the first commissioners of Kapiʻolani Park, and an original board member of the Honolulu Rapid Transit Company (**VIII-1**). He was also instrumental in the overthrow of Queen Liliʻuokalani in 1893, helping to write the constitution of the Hawaiian republic and participating in the negotiations in Washington for annexation.

Notice the flowers and trees here: hibiscus plants and monkeypod trees (*Samanea saman*).

Kapahulu Avenue is thought of as the Diamond Head end of Waikīkī proper. This street is named for the district through which it passes *mauka* of here. *Kapahulu* has two very different interpretations in Hawaiian: 'the worn-out soil' and 'a feather garment.' The latter interpretation may have referred to a feather garment worn by King Lunalilo, who owned a tract of land in the area.

Hibiscus

Cross Ala Wai Boulevard to the *ʻEwa* side of Kapahulu Avenue.

 Waikīkī-Kapahulu Public Library
9

Waikīkī-Kapahulu Library

The library is one of Waikīkī's architectural gems. Its exterior walls are made of locally hewn sandstone blocks. The ceiling is of imported cedar; the interior doors, the reading bench, and children's tables are of native *koa* wood. This building, designed by Lemmon and French, opened its doors to the public in 1952. (The first Waikīkī library was located in a wooden cottage on the grounds of Jefferson School [**VI-7**].)

In the entryway, view the cement sculpture of an outrigger canoe on the wall.

Behind Waikīkī-Kapahulu Library is another library—the Hawaiʻi State Library for the Blind and the Physically Handicapped. This is why the "walk" signal at the crosswalk beeps.

The street *mauka-ʻEwa* of the libraries leads to the Ala Wai Golf Course (**I-1**).

Cross Kapahulu Avenue to Pākī Avenue (an extension of Ala Wai Boulevard). Walk Diamond Head along the *mauka* side of Pākī.

LOCAL LIFE TODAY IN WAIKĪKĪ ✣ **WALK VI**

10   Waikīkī Fire Station: Station No. 7

Waikīkī Fire Station No. 7

Its sleek, clean lines make this building appear quite modern, but it was actually constructed in 1927, a year after the library diagonally across the way. It was designed by architects Davis and Fishbourne, and is surely one of the loveliest firehouses to be found anywhere.

Waikīkī firemen

In front of the fire station are several interesting plants:
- Spider lily plants.
- A large monkeypod tree. Its wood is used in many of the wooden bowls and wood carvings sold as souvenirs of Hawai'i.
- Papaya trees.
- Ti, *kī* in Hawaiian. The many varieties of the ti plant are widely used in ornamental plantings around the islands. For the Hawaiians, though, the *kī* was used for house thatching, food wrappings, *hula* skirts, and sandals. The *kī* root was cooked and used for food and distilled liquor. The ti leaf is still used in present-day Hawaiian cooking: the leaf is wrapped around butterfish, which is then cooked and served in its wrapper. Be sure to try real Hawaiian food before you leave the islands!
- Banana trees.

Banana tree

- *'Ape*, often called "elephant ears," which is closely related to taro (*kalo* in Hawaiian). The *'ape* you see here is reminiscent of the hundreds of acres of wet taro fields in Waikīkī before the diversion of the three streams and the dredging of the Ala Wai Canal in the 1920s (**Walk II**).

Continue along Pākī Avenue, lined with monkeypod trees.

WALK VI ❖ LOCAL LIFE TODAY IN WAIKĪKĪ

Pākī Avenue, Pākī Park, and Pākī Playground

This park is used for picnicking and as a playground for neighborhood children. Notice the exceptionally soft rubber matting on the ground under the playground equipment.

This park, the street, and Pākī Hale, 'house' (**VI-17**), are named for a high chief of Maui named Pākī, who was the father of Princess Bernice Pauahi Bishop (1831–1884).

It is said that Duke Kahanamoku, Hawai'i's best-known athlete, was born on this street, in a house his family called *Haleakalā*. However, he spent most of his childhood in *Kālia*, on the 'Ewa end of Waikīkī (**IX-1**), at his mother's family home.

Continue to the Diamond Head-*mauka* corner of Monsarrat and Pākī avenues.

Queen Kapi'olani Hibiscus Garden

This lovely garden was founded by the Outdoor Circle in 1926 as Kapi'olani Nursery. The Outdoor Circle is the very organization we can thank for the banning of billboards in Hawai'i in 1927. Thank you, Outdoor Circle!

Queen Kapi'olani Hibiscus Garden

Since its inception, the garden has had many faces. During World War II the nursery was a victory garden; in the 1960s, it was known as the Kapi'olani Hibiscus Garden; then, in the 1970s, when the nursery officially became part of Kapi'olani Park, it was dedicated as Queen Kapi'olani Garden; and now, its full, blended name: Queen Kapi'olani Hibiscus Garden.

The garden is always open and displays other plants as well as the many varieties of hibiscus. Walk along the grass paths to view:

- Cotton, which is related to the hibiscus.
- *Hau*, also related to the hibiscus. In the course of its life, the *hau* blossom displays three different colors: yellow upon opening in the morning, then bright orange during the day, and red-brown when it drops at the end of the day. Is this an allegory of a person's life? The *hau* tree had many traditional uses: its tough but lightweight wood was used for making canoe outriggers; its fibers were made into rope; and its sap and flowers were used medicinally.
- Plumeria is a popular flower used in *lei* despite the fact that it is also known as the "graveyard flower," since it is widely planted in cemeteries.
- *Laua'e*, or *maile*-scented, fern. When crushed, the leaves give off a perfume similar to that of the native *maile* vine. The midrib of the *laua'e* is used as a backbone for *lei po'o* 'head *lei*' and *lei pāpale* 'hat *lei*.'

On the 'Ewa side of the garden are tables in the shade of the *hau* trees.

LOCAL LIFE TODAY IN WAIKĪKĪ ✦ **WALK VI**

Local folklore relates that the large boulders at the Diamond Head end of the garden are the guardian stones of the garden, offering spiritual healing to the Hawaiian people. The stones were brought from Tahiti in the fourteenth century and serve as *kāhuna* or "guardian" stones (see **IX-15** for more information about the *kāhun*a and Kāhuna Stones).

Laua'e

 Monsarrat Avenue

Monsarrat Avenue is named either for Marcus Cumming Monsarrat, an Irishman who came to Hawai'i in 1850, or his son, Judge James Melville Monsarrat, advisor to the monarchy.

Cross Monsarrat, continue Diamond Head-*makai* along Pākī.

 Waikīkī School

One block *mauka* of Pākī is another elementary school, smaller than Jefferson, with just over three hundred students in kindergarten through sixth grade.

Continue along Pākī. Diagonally across is one of the parking lots for Kapi'olani Park.

People's open market

 **People's Open Market—
If It's Wednesday Morning,
You're in Luck!**

On Wednesday mornings from 10:00 to 11:00 A.M., this parking lot is transformed into a bustling farmers' market, where homegrown produce is sold at prices lower than in supermarkets. Look for (Japanese) long eggplants, Maui onions, Mānoa lettuce, apple bananas, mangoes, star fruit, and various Asian vegetables. This is your chance to enjoy your fruits and veggies!

Papaya at the people's open market

WALK VI ✣ LOCAL LIFE TODAY IN WAIKĪKĪ

 Diamond Head Community Gardens

Halfway down the block, on the Diamond Head side of Pākī, is a community garden. This garden is a city project of small garden plots where local residents of nearby apartments and houses lovingly cultivate vegetables for their own uses.

Continue along on Pākī Avenue.

 Pākī Hale
3840 Pākī Avenue

Pākī Hale

The two-story building (plus its peekaboo third-story window), part of Honolulu's Department of Parks and Recreation, is available for use by community organizations. It was originally home to the Carl Winstedt family, dating to 1918, with major renovations in 1925. The property was purchased by the City and County of Honolulu in 1976 and dedicated as a recreation facility in 1992.

Notice the beautiful Spanish tile roof. Even the garage is exceptional!

 Kapi'olani Park

At this end of Pākī, also on the Diamond Head side, are tennis courts and an archery range, both part of Kapi'olani Park (**VII**).

Notice the curved row of stately date palm trees on the other side of Pākī. These trees are the last remnants of a nineteenth-century racetrack (**VII-6**).

This is the Diamond Head-*makai* end of Kapi'olani Park.

This is the end of **Walk VI**. If you wish to continue, choose one of the two following walks:

• **Walk VII**, Kapi'olani Park and Honolulu Zoo, which begins at the intersection of Monsarrat and Kapahulu avenues; or
• **Walk VIII**, Foot of Diamond Head, which begins at the Waikīkī Aquarium on Kalākaua Avenue.

Walk VII

· Kapi'olani Park and
Honolulu Zoo ·

Queen Kapi'olani

Walk VII
Kapi'olani Park and Honolulu Zoo
Diamond Head-*makai* end of Waikīkī

🕒 **TIME:** 1 hour or more, if you like the zoo!
➪ **DISTANCE:** 0.5 mile (0.8 kilometer)

O N THIS WALK YOU CAN MEANDER THROUGH KAPI'OLANI PARK AND THE HONOLULU ZOO, STOPPING OCCASIONALLY TO CONTEMPLATE HISTORIC SITES, SUCH AS A REPLICA OF A TROLLEY STOP AND A RACETRACK LONG GONE.

The district where the park and zoo are now located was known as *Kāneloa*, meaning 'tall man.' Kāne was also the name of one of the most important Hawaiian gods. 🌺

▶ **BEGIN WALK:** *There is no official entrance to Kapi'olani Park, but a convenient place to start is at the intersection of Monsarrat and Kalākaua avenues, Diamond Head of the zoo entrance, perhaps at the benches near the bandstand. Take a few moments to sit in the shade of the ironwood trees and read about the park's interesting history.*

This is a loop trail.

Monsarrat Avenue is named either for Marcus Cumming Monsarrat, an Irishman who came to Hawai'i in 1850, or his son, Judge James Melville Monsarrat, advisor to the monarchy.

 Kapi'olani Park
Honolulu Marathon

Kapi'olani Park, a 100-acre recreation area, is named for Queen Kapi'olani ('arch of heaven'), who lived from 1834 (or 1836—accounts differ as to the year of her birth) to 1899. She and her husband, King Kalākaua, reigned from 1874 to 1891.

King Kalākaua presented the park as a gift to the people of his kingdom in 1877, and it was officially dedicated to the queen on Kamehameha Day, June 11, of that year. It was the first major public park in the kingdom.

According to information from the Kamehameha Celebration Commission, "Kamehameha the Great was born somewhere between 1748 and 1761 in North Kohala on the island of Hawai'i. Although the exact date is unknown, by royal Proclamation in 1871 of King Kamehameha V in honor of his grandfather, June 11 of each year was designated as a holiday to honor the life and times of Hawai'i's greatest statesman, warrior and king." The holiday is celebrated with festivities in Kapi'olani Park and an elaborate parade through Honolulu. Kamehameha Day

WALK VII
Kapi'olani Park and Honolulu Zoo

Diamond Head-*makai* end of Waikīkī

VII-1	Kapi'olani Park
	Honolulu Marathon
VII-2	Queen Kapi'olani Statue
VII-3	Kapi'olani Bandstand
VII-4	Time Capsule
VII-5	Joggers' Rest
	Trolley Stop and Shelter
VII-6	*Racetrack*
VII-7	Waikīkī Shell Amphitheater
	Hula Show
VII-8	*Makee Island*
	Makee Road
VII-9	Mahatma Gandhi Statue
VII-10	Hawaiian Burial Memorial
	Kāhi Hāli'a Aloha
VII-11	Honolulu Zoo

is even celebrated in Washington D.C., in the Capitol Building, where a bronze statue of Kamehameha I is festooned with *lei*, accompanied by Hawaiian chanting and dancing.

Archibald Cleghorn, Princess Ka'iulani's father, helped design the park, including the trees. Greater Kapi'olani Park includes Kapi'olani Park Beach and Queen's Surf Beach.

The parklands were created by the Kapi'olani Park Association, a collaboration of royal grants from the crown and two hundred private members. The park originally included the land 'Ewa of this point, now occupied by the Honolulu Zoo.

In its early days, the park contained numerous lily and goldfish ponds, dotted by islands planted with palm trees, hibiscus, and crotons. The Royal Hawaiian Band, the oldest municipal band in the country, performed atop one of the islands, much to the delight of picnickers. You may still hear the band most Sundays at 2:00 P.M.

During the Spanish-American War (April to August 1898), the first military camps in Hawai'i were established in Kapi'olani Park, where they remained until 1907. The military troops actually marched from Honolulu Harbor to Kapi'olani Park! *Camp McKinley* opened in 1898 and *Camp Otis* soon followed. Today, nothing remains of those temporary military sites. The military moved to Fort DeRussy, on the 'Ewa side of Waikīkī (**Walk II**).

Kapi'olani Park also boasts accommodating one of the first airfields in Hawai'i, including the launching site of a balloon ascent in 1889.

In the 1920s the park's ponds were

filled in with dredgings from the Ala Wai Canal project. It was claimed at the time that the park was falling into disrepair due to poor maintenance by the territorial government that took control of Hawai'i in 1900.

Kapi'olani Park is very popular today for picnicking and various sports: baseball, football, soccer, rugby, and other more exotic games. More impressively, the park is one of Honolulu joggers' favorite routes, measuring 1.8 miles; adding the zoo to the route increases the distance to 2.2 miles. There are also exercise stations and a joggers' course along the way.

Along Pākī Avenue (**VI-11** to **18**), *mauka* of here, are archery ranges, a tennis court, and a lifeguard station, which was moved there in 1976 when the Natatorium was condemned (**VIII-3**).

On the second Sunday of each December, this tranquil setting is transformed into the home of a major world event: the Honolulu Marathon, which began in 1973 and has grown to a world-class run with approximately thirty thousand runners of all levels. To aid in the training of local runners, the Honolulu Marathon Clinic meets at Kapi'olani Park at 7:30 A.M. every Sunday beginning in March. The original marathon distance, 26.2 miles, was based on the distance from Athens to Marathon, a city northeast of Athens. The marathon is founded on the legend that Phidippides ran from Marathon to Athens to announce the victory of Athens over the Persians in 490 B.C.E.

Walk along Kalākaua, toward Diamond Head. On your way, notice the interesting pattern in the crosswalk:

this is a Hawaiian tapa design. Tapa is a local fabric made from native plants, with designs similar to the one in the crosswalk placed on the fabric. In the coffee tables of the Tapa Tower of the Hilton Hawaiian Village (II-12), there is an excellent display and explanation of tapa making.

 Queen Kapiʻolani Statue

Queen Kapiʻolani statue

The bronze statue of Queen Kapiʻolani was created by artist Holly Young. The plaque is inscribed with the queen's legacy: *Kūlia I Ka Nuʻu*, 'Strive for the Highest.' In 1890, the queen left a bequest to Kapiʻolani Maternity Home, now known as Kapiʻolani Medical Center for Women and Children.

 Kapiʻolani Bandstand

The beautiful Victorian-style gazebo, which replaced an earlier bandstand, was designed by David Ayer of the architectural firm of Stringer and Tusher. The area around the bandstand has been landscaped

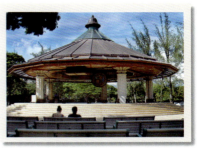

Kapiʻolani bandstand

recently with ponds and lakes to reflect earlier days of Kapiʻolani Park, before the Ala Wai Canal.

The bandstand, dedicated on Independence Day in 2000, is a fifteen-sided polygon with a sloped copper roof topped with circular glass skylights and a copper cupola. The roof is installed with roll-down walls for night security and sound control. The Royal Hawaiian Band, which has its office in the back of the Waikīkī Shell amphitheater, holds its concerts here on Sunday afternoons. Check newspaper listings for concert schedules.

 Time Capsule

Diamond Head of the bandstand is a time capsule that celebrates the

Bandstand and time capsule

100th anniversary of Kapi'olani Park. The capsule is to be opened on June 11, 2077. It's impossible to imagine what Waikīkī will look like then!

Time capsule sign

 **Joggers' Rest
Trolley Stop and Shelter**

The quaint-looking structure on Kalākaua Avenue is a replica of a trolley stop. Today it is a joggers' rest stop. Kapi'olani Park offers a long course and short course with exercise stations along the way.

A similar Victorian shelter was installed concurrently with the opening of the Aquarium in 1904 (**VIII-1**). Interestingly, the owners of the Honolulu Rapid Transit Company also owned the Aquarium. This site for the shelter

Joggers' rest

was chosen in the hope of luring more passengers to this end of Waikīkī.

The trolley stop was restored in 1975 and affectionately renamed "Joggers' Rest." Near the shelter is a water fountain, a welcome sight indeed for anyone (you?) jogging or walking in the hot sun.

Around the end of the nineteenth century and beginning of the twentieth century, two local transportation systems coexisted: the Hawaiian Tramways Company, a horse-tram system, and the Honolulu Rapid Transit Company, which provided an electric trolley.

A Waikīkī trolley service has been restored, with reproductions of San Francisco cable cars that were introduced in April 1986.

Stroll away from the beach, diagonally across the park toward the Waikīkī Shell. Just past the tennis courts, on the 'Ewa side, you will see a group of palm trees.

 Racetrack

The curved row of date palm trees formerly lined the 'Ewa curve of the Kapi'olani Park racetrack, complete with a truly grand grandstand. The racetrack was designed by Captain James Makee, who was originally from Scotland. A former island in the park was named after him (**VII-8**). Horse racing was extremely popular in the late nineteenth century, especially the Rosita Cup, an annual event on Kamehameha Day, June 11. Due to excessive betting, the park commissioner banned horse racing, demolishing both the racetrack and

Palms at former racetrack

grandstand in the 1920s. Horse racing was soon replaced by polo games.

A dozen stately date palms continue to outline the Diamond Head end of the racetrack.

Walk around the back of the amphitheater.

Waikīkī Shell Amphitheater Hula Show

The entrance to the Waikīkī Shell amphitheater is on Monsarrat Avenue. This outdoor theater, built in 1953 and seating eight thousand, really looks like a shell, especially from the back as you walk toward it. It is used for diverse events, ranging from high school and community college graduations (it was even used at one time for University of Hawai'i at Mānoa commencement ceremonies, where the author received her doctorate in linguistics in 1979) to Hawaiian-music concerts by local entertainers and the Honolulu Symphony. If a concert is scheduled during your stay in Waikīkī, do attend. You'll never forget the event under the stars. The best and least-expensive seats are on the lawn! Come early; bring food, a blanket, and friends; and picnic on the grass before the event begins.

You may have seen postcards with five *hula* dancers, each one holding up the individual letters in Hawai'i. That was the "Kodak moment" tourists snapped away at for sixty-five years.

The *Kodak Hula Show*, and more recently the *Pleasant Hawaiian Hula Show*, was held in a smaller area *makai* of "the Shell." Originally established in 1937 at the Sans Souci Beach (**VIII-5**), then moving to the Shell thirty years later, the show was the longest continuously operating *hula* show in Hawai'i—sixty-five years of *hula*! It is estimated that twenty million people, most of them with cameras, have seen the *hula* shows. Mae Akeo Brown, the dancer who holds the record for the longest duration with the show, joined the show in 1938 as a little girl. Ironically, sixty-five years is also the interval between the time that *hula* was banned in 1820 by the missionaries and when it was revived by the Merrie Monarch, King Kalākaua.

Hula performed here was mainly Hawaiian, in the style of King Kalākaua's time (1836–1891), with some Tahitian-style dancing. Missionaries succeeded in banning the *hula* in 1820 because of the misperception of this graceful, dignified dance form. *Hula* shows are held at various locations in Waikīkī and at the Bishop Museum in Kalihi.

Walk back across Kapi'olani Park to the Honolulu Zoo at the corner of Kapahulu and Monsarrat avenues, taking pleasure in watching the picnickers, athletes, and strollers enjoying the park. And listen to the wild screeching of the gibbons in the zoo!

Makee Island c. 1890 (Hawai'i State Archives)

8 Makee Island
Makee Road

Before the zoo was established, a large man-made island, *Makee Island*, was located here, covering most of the present-day zoo. Captain James Makee, a resourceful and talented Scotsman, was a whaling ship's captain, rancher, and commercial developer in the mid-1800s. In the 1860s he established Rose Ranch on the slopes of Haleakalā on Maui, developing it into a cattle ranch estate where the Hawaiian monarchy enjoyed being wined and dined. In 1876, Makee was one of the organizers of Kapi'olani Park Association and one of the developers of the long-gone racetrack in Kapi'olani Park (**VII-6**).

Makee Road, a short diagonal road 'Ewa of the zoo, off Kapahulu Avenue, is named for him. Makee Road was almost completely absorbed by Kapahulu Avenue when Kapahulu was extended.

9 Mahatma Gandhi Statue

Mahatma Gandhi statue

The banyan trees shade a statue of Indian nationalist and spiritual leader Mohandas K. Gandhi. Over the years many animals from India have been presented to the zoo (**VII-11**). As a continuing gesture of harmony, this statue and these words of Gandhi welcome visitors:

> It is possible to live in Peace.

Gandhi, who preached nonviolent protest, lived from 1869 to 1948. He was killed in Delhi, India, by an assassin's bullet while on his way to evening prayers.

Walk to the corner of Kapahulu and Monsarrat avenues to see the unusual-looking lava structure.

Hawaiian Burial Memorial
Kāhi Hāli'a Aloha

Hawaiian Burial Memorial

As a result of the continuing disruption of the ground at Waikīkī from improvements begun in the late 1990s, many bones of native Hawaiians were uncovered. Modern-day lineal descendants of these Hawaiians dedicated this eight-sided pyramid-shaped mound to provide a final, dignified resting place for their ancestors. Kāhi Hāli'a Aloha, 'The Place of Loving Remembrance,' is a burial place of respect for the Hawaiians of old who lived and died in Waikīkī.

The architectural design is quite intriguing: old lava stones at the bottom of the wall and new lava above, topped by a torch, which is lit whenever another body is interred. Benches are strategically placed inside the memorial for rest and contemplation for the lineal descendants. The green and red ti plants have been planted as protection to ward off evil spirits.

Kāhi Hāli'a Aloha bronze plaque with lei

As stated in the mayor's office news release, "The Memorial is the first of its kind to offer permanent and dignified protection to generations of Hawaiian ancestral remains unearthed and/or repatriated from museum collections across the nation."

The bronze plaque is a message to us from the lineal descendants.

Honolulu Zoo

The main entrance to the Honolulu Zoo is on Kalākaua Avenue between Kapahulu and Monsarrat avenues at the banyan and monkeypod trees.

The forty-acre zoo, with more than twelve hundred mammals, birds, and reptiles, is the largest and best zoo for twenty-three hundred miles around!

WALK VII ✣ KAPIʻOLANI PARK AND HONOLULU ZOO

And it is the only zoo in the U.S. that originated from a Royal Land Grant. Initially part of Kapiʻolani Park, it included King Kalākaua's exotic birds as original residents. They were soon joined by peacocks and flora from Golden Gate Park in San Francisco. It is very likely that Princess Kaʻiulani's peacocks (**V-1**) were donated to the zoo at that time.

Honolulu Zoo

The first park administrator, Ben Hollinger, brought in the first monkey, bear, lion cubs, and imported birds beginning in 1914. Only two years later, the zoo's character changed dramatically with the introduction of an African elephant, Daisy, who lived until 1933. How all of Honolulu loved Daisy! She particularly enjoyed carrying children around on her back. The zoo's current Asian elephants, Mari, born in 1975, and Vaigai, born in 1985, were presented as gifts to the zoo from the children of India.

During the depression and World War II, the zoo fell into disrepair. Only the bird collection prospered during that period, due to the efforts of E. H. Lewis, an ornithologist from California. For a while, the zoo was understandably known as Kapiʻolani Bird Park. In 1974, the zoo was revitalized, with many new animals being added, including a camel, elephants, chimpanzees, and deer. In 1992 the zoo was redesigned to its present character, emphasizing the African savannah, a tropical forest, islands of the Pacific, and a children's zoo.

You may have heard that there are no snakes in Hawaiʻi except those in the Honolulu Zoo. Actually, there is a type of blind snake that came into the islands in the 1930s, but it is extremely timid and absolutely harmless. The Honolulu Zoo imported its first snake in 1971: a small red snake from Florida, no longer living. By law, only two snakes, both of the same sex, are allowed to reside in the zoo at one time!

The zoo is open every day except Christmas and New Year's Day from 9:00 A.M. to 4:30 P.M. During the summer, free concerts are held every Wednesday at 6:00 P.M., with the gates opening at 4:30. For a special treat, inquire about the overnight program, "Snooze in the Zoo"—surely something you'll never forget!

This is the end of **Walk VII**. If you wish to continue walking, connect here with **Walk VIII**, Foot of Diamond Head.

Diamond Head

Walk VIII
· Foot of Diamond Head ·

Hau Tree Lānai restaurant

Walk VIII
Foot of Diamond Head
Extreme Diamond Head end of Waikīkī Beach, including slope of Diamond Head

⏱ **TIME:** 1.5 to 2 hours
➪ **DISTANCE:** 1.5 miles (2.4 kilometers)

THIS WALK GOES THROUGH THE HISTORIC DISTRICT, OR *'ILI*, OF *KAPUA*, 'THE FLOWER,' ALONG THE OCEAN AT THE FOOT OF DIAMOND HEAD. In 1823, Kamehameha II presented *Kapua* as a tribute to a member of his court, Chief Iona Pehu. More history of *Kapua* is related at stop **VIII-4** of this walk.

After the *Mahele* of 1848, when royal land was distributed, more and more beaches and homes in this area came to be owned by European and American *haole*. (Today, *haole* refers to Caucasians, but originally, it meant any foreigner.) From Kapahulu Avenue continuing Diamond Head, landowners recorded on an 1895 map of the area were:

Magoon Brothers	A. Herbert
E. S. Cunha	J. B. Castle
C. H. Brown	Westervelt
H. M. von Holt	W. G. Irwin
S. N. Castle	G. W. Macfarlane
McInerny	G. P. Castle
F. M. Hatch	

Some of these landowners never developed their properties, but others, such as the McInerny and J. B. Castle families, built beautiful beachfront mansions. Visible remnants of those two homes still exist (**VIII-6** and **8**). Today all beaches in Hawai'i are public property and completely accessible, except for those at military reservations.

The first condominium building went up at this end of Waikīkī: a twelve-story structure at 3019 Kalākaua Avenue, built in 1961. ❧

> ➤ **BEGIN WALK:** *This walk starts at the Waikīkī Aquarium, just below Diamond Head, continuing toward Diamond Head along the beach and stopping at various places of interest on the slope of Diamond Head.*
>
> *The pine-like ironwood trees lining Kalākaua Avenue were planted by Archibald Cleghorn (**V-7**) in 1890. Cleghorn, the first commissioner of parks and a governor of Hawai'i, was the husband of Princess Likelike. Near the Diamond Head end of this street are several shower trees that bloom pink and white in the spring. The rainbow shower tree is Honolulu's official tree.*

WALK VIII
Foot of Diamond Head

Extreme Diamond Head end of Waikīkī Beach, including slope of Diamond Head.

VIII-1	Waikīkī Aquarium
VIII-2	Queen's Surf Beach
	Deering-Holmes Estate
	Heiau Kupalaha
VIII-3	War Memorial Natatorium
VIII-4	Kapua Channel
	Kapua
VIII-5	Sans Souci Beach
	Sans Souci Hotel
VIII-6	New Otani Kaimana Beach Hotel
	Hau Tree Lānai Restaurant
	McInerny Estate
VIII-7	Outrigger Canoe Club
VIII-8	Elks Club
	Macfarlane Home
	C. N. Arnold Home and Park Beach Hotel
	Castle Estate/Kainalu
VIII-9	Kalehuawehe
VIII-10	Dillingham Fountain
VIII-11	Poni Mō'ī Street
VIII-12	Diamond Head
VIII-13	Mākālei Beach Park and Mākālei Place
VIII-14	La Pietra Hawai'i School for Girls
	Heiau Papa'ena'ena

WALK VIII ✢ FOOT OF DIAMOND HEAD

 Waikīkī Aquarium

The Waikīkī Aquarium is the third oldest public aquarium in the United States and the oldest in the Pacific Basin. Since 1919, the Aquarium has been an integral part of the University of Hawai'i, collaborating on research and information. It was established in 1904 by James B. Castle, Charles M. Cooke, and Lorrin Thurston, all local businessmen who were descendants of missionaries, and built on land bequeathed by Castle, whose home was close by (**VIII-8**).

Waikīkī Aquarium

Coincidentally (and interestingly!), Messieurs Castle, Cooke, and Thurston were board members of the Honolulu Rapid Transit Company, which had recently established a new electric trolley line from downtown Honolulu to Waikīkī (**VII-5**). By locating the Aquarium so far Diamond Head, the board members hoped to lure more passengers to ride to the terminus of the trolley line. Today, the Waikīkī Trolley has inherited that privilege.

Originally located in Kapi'olani Beach Park, just *'Ewa* of its present site, the Aquarium moved in 1955 to its present building of locally hewn sandstone, which is built virtually on a living reef. The Aquarium, which is open every day except Christmas Day, contains more than 2,500 organisms and 420 species of aquatic plant and life forms. Its highlight is the endangered Hawaiian monk seal.

Naupaka

Notice the lovely flora to the right of the Aquarium building: the beautiful *'ulu* 'breadfruit' tree, red and green ti, and the low-lying *naupaka*. The *naupaka*, a native beach plant, is found on other Pacific islands as well. If you look closely for its small white flower, you will actually see a half flower. There are many legends concerning this half blossom. One legend involves a maiden who became suspicious of her lover's faithfulness. As a test, she tore the flower in two and gave him one half, telling him to bring back a complete flower as proof of his love. Her lover was unsuccessful.

Another legend involves a related mountain plant that bears an identical flower but has drastically different leaves. In this legend, a Hawaiian *Romeo and Julie*t, lovers who had been forbidden to marry because of their different backgrounds and social classes decided to die together. The Hawaiian gods turned the woman into the *naupaka kahakai* (by the sea) and

FOOT OF DIAMOND HEAD ✦ **WALK VIII**

the man into the *naupaka kuahiwi* (mountain), joining their love in spirit.

 **Queen's Surf Beach
Deering-Holmes Estate
Heiau Kupalaha**

Queen's Surf Beach is named in honor of Queen Kapi'olani, whose name was also given to nearby Kapi'olani Park.

The first nonroyal residence here belonged to the Charles Deering family, and then, in the 1930s, to Christopher Holmes. During World War II, the *Deering-Holmes Estate*, as it was later known, served as a conference center for President Roosevelt. In 1946 the mansion was converted into the *Queen's Surf Restaurant*. Its entertainment area, known as the *Barefoot Bar*, was a popular center for Hawaiian music and dance. Although the City and County of Honolulu obtained the land in 1953, the restaurant was allowed to continue operations. In 1961 the Spencecliff Corporation leased the restaurant for ten years, and *Queen's Surf* became known for its beach *lū'au*. When the Spencecliff lease expired in 1971, the mansion-turned-restaurant was demolished to create more open space along the beach.

Heiau Kupalaha was a religious structure located at Queen's Surf Beach. It is thought that it operated in conjunction with *Heiau Papa'ena'ena* (**VIII-14**) on the slope of Diamond Head.

The surfing area here is not called Queens; Queens is actually off Waikīkī Beach Center.

3 **War Memorial Natatorium**

The War Memorial, as is carved overhead on the arch, is known locally as the Natatorium, which is simply a fancy name for "swimming pool." It was inaugurated on August 24, 1927, which was, coincidentally (or was it contrived?), the anniversary of the birth of Duke Kahanamoku, Hawai'i's stellar Olympic swimmer (**IX-1** and **17**). The War Memorial was dedicated to local soldiers who fought in World War I. Across from the arch is a large lava (local stone) boulder with the Roll of Honor inscribed with their names.

War Memorial Natatorium

Land for the War Memorial project was obtained by the city from the William G. Irwin Estate. The architect of the home, which was built in 1899 and razed in the 1920s, was Charles W. Dickey, also the architect for the only remaining Halekūlani building (**IX-5**). He is still well known for the design of the breeze-catching roof slope, the "Dickey roof."

The Natatorium structure was designed by architect Louis P. Hobart, who also designed San Francisco's Grace Cathedral and various structures in Golden Gate Park. Notice the graceful carvings and moldings surrounding the Natatorium entrance: garlands, eagles, urns, and the Hawaiian standard and motto. The entire façade

WALK VIII ✦ FOOT OF DIAMOND HEAD

was recently renovated. As you stand under the arch, look down to view the geometric design in the drain grate.

The pool measures 100 meters by 40 meters, and the structure provides seating for six thousand spectators. It was in this very pool that Duke Kahanamoku, who went on to win Olympic gold and silver medals in swimming, swam! To this day the Natatorium remains the largest saltwater pool in the United States. However, due to its deteriorating condition, the pool portion of the Natatorium is closed.

Look for outrigger canoes on the Diamond Head side of the Memorial. Canoe teams practice in this area (and may also be seen all along the Ala Wai Canal, **Walk I**).

There are several interesting trees in front of the War Memorial:
- *Hau* trees growing on a trellis. Notice the flowers that open yellow, turn orange, and drop to the ground a brown-red color.
- Three banyan trees.
- Coconut trees (The metal rings around the trunks are rat guards.)

Kapua Channel
Kapua

As mentioned in the introduction to this walk, this entire area was once known as *Kapua*, 'the flower.' Kapua Channel is visible offshore, Diamond Head of the Natatorium. In 1904 the Commercial Pacific Cable was laid in the channel. This underground cable contained telephone and telegraph lines linking San Francisco and Honolulu.

During the 1853 smallpox epidemic, which killed thousands of Hawaiians, *Kapua* was used as a quarantine station for newly arrived visitors.

The protected shore and channel of *Kapua* formed an important harbor for this part of O'ahu. *Kapua* was also the favorite surfing area of one of Kamehameha I's wives, Ka'ahumanu. Legend relates that Ka'ahumanu surfed and lamented in *Kapua* after she and her lover were discovered. He was sacrificed on a sacrificial *heiau*, 'religious structure,' at Diamond Head (**VIII-14**).

At least seven *heiau* were said to be located in Waikīkī. This one, *Kapua*, was a *heiau po'o kanaka*, or *luakini* type, a place where human sacrifices were offered. Conflicting reports tell of varying sizes. According to J. Gilbert McAllister's 1933 *Archaeology of Oahu*, this *heiau* was small, only 240 square feet; but George S. Kanahele's *Waikīkī 100 B.C. to 1900 A.D.: An Untold Story* says it was very large, measuring 240 by 240 feet. (You choose which one to believe!)

This *heiau*, along with most other *heiau*, was probably destroyed sometime after 1819 when traditional Hawaiian religion was challenged by Kamehameha II. Soon after the death of Kamehameha I in 1819, his wives and son (Kamehameha II) set about to abolish the ways of their traditional religion. This did not come about overnight: Ka'ahumanu, Kamehameha's favorite wife, had already challenged and, thereby, had broken the *kapu* not only of eating with men, but also eating food (bananas) forbidden to women. This change opened the way for the Christian religion that was brought to Hawai'i by the missionaries the following year, 1820.

Kapua is also remembered as the place where Kaolahaka, a chief from the Big Island of Hawai'i, was sacrificed on suspicion of being a spy. *Kapua* was well known as a place of bone-breaking wrestling.

A *heiau* in Waimea Valley on the North Shore of O'ahu still exists today. Considered to be the biggest *heiau* ever, at four acres, Pu'u o Mahuka, 'Hill of Escape,' dates to the 1600s.

Continue Diamond Head along the beach.

Sans Souci Beach
Sans Souci Hotel

The beach in front of the New Otani Kaimana Beach Hotel and neighboring Sans Souci Apartments is known as the Sans Souci Beach, named for the *Sans Souci Hotel*, which once stood here. In actuality, this beach was part of *Kapua*. Sans Souci (French for 'carefree') is named for the palace of Frederick II (Frederick the Great), built in the mid-eighteenth century in Potsdam, Germany.

In 1884 Allen Herbert from Sweden attempted to turn his home into a hotel. However, it wasn't until 1893 that George Lycurgus, a Greek immigrant who is best known as the developer of the Volcano House on the island of Hawai'i, leased the hotel and ran a successful hostelry. Mr. Lycurgus died in 1970 at the age of 101!

This area was extremely popular during the 1890s, and the *Sans Souci Hotel*, which consisted of small bungalows with thatched roofs, became one of Waikīkī's leading inns—arguably Waikīkī's first famous hotel. During World War I the hotel was purchased by Mr. and Mrs. Charles Hartwell. who replaced the original building, retaining only the original foundation.

The spreading *hau* tree, which has been in this spot for more than 100 years, lends its name to the Hau Tree Lānai restaurant (next stop). *Hau* belongs to the Malvaeceae (mallow) family, which includes the hibiscus. In the course of its life (one day!), the *hau* blossom displays three different colors: yellow upon opening, then bright orange, and finally red-brown when it drops. The *hau* tree had many traditional uses: its rough but lightweight wood was used for making canoe outriggers; its fiber was made into rope; and its sap and flowers were used medicinally. It is quite possible that Robert Louis Stevenson, who was a frequent guest to this area, wrote while sitting under this tree! In 1893 he wrote:

> If anyone desires such old fashioned things as lovely scenery, quiet, pure air, clear sea water, good food, and heavenly sunsets hung out before his eyes over the Pacific and the distant hills of Wai'anae, I recommend him cordially to the Sans Souci.

Sans Souci Beach

There is, today, a Sans Souci Apartments nearby: a different building, with different owners, but perhaps with the same ambience—it's up to you. The original *Hula Show* began here at the Sans Souci Beach in 1937. The show, which moved to an area near the Waikīkī amphitheater in 1969, closed in 2002.

6 New Otani Kaimana Beach Hotel / Hau Tree Lānai Restaurant / McInerny Estate

The white railing separating the Hau Tree Lānai restaurant from the beach may be part of the original fence of the *McInerny Estate*, located here in the early part of the twentieth century. McInerny was a retail merchant who established his first store on the corner of Merchant and Fort streets in downtown Honolulu. If you look closely on the top of the railing, there is a plaque that reads:

> Kaimana Beach Hamburger Stand
> 4th anniversary of its demise
> 18th October 1989

Hau Tree Lānai Restaurant

Always history in the making. Yes, those were delicious hamburgers!

The name of this hotel reflects the interesting blend of cultures in Hawai'i: Otani is the name of the Japanese owner and the name of several hotels in Japan; *Kaimana*, although now a Hawaiian word, was borrowed from the English *diamond*.

Please respect the sign on the beach:

> KAPU [taboo]
> Private Property
> Keep off fence and seawall

Do not attempt to cross through the water to the next stop. Please go back to Kalākaua Avenue and pass in front of the two clubs (Outrigger Canoe Club and Elks Club) on your way toward Diamond Head (**VIII-12**).

7 Outrigger Canoe Club

If you have taken **Walk III** or **IX**, you have visited the original site of this club: the present Outrigger Waikīkī Hotel, related in name only.

The Outrigger Canoe Club, at its original location, was organized in 1908 to revive the ancient Hawaiian sport of surfing. Its most outstanding member was Alexander Hume Ford. Mr. Ford is often referred to as a visionary because of his foresight in reestablishing the dying, but vital, sport of surfing. He was also the founder of the magazine *Mid-Pacific* and the still-active Hawaiian Trail and Mountain Club.

Leasing land from the Elks Club (next stop), the Outrigger Canoe Club moved to its present location in 1964. Part of the beach fronting the club was created with sand removed during excavation of the building's foundation.

FOOT OF DIAMOND HEAD ✢ **WALK VIII**

J. B. Castle residence, Kainalu, Waikīkī c. 1901 (C. J. Hedemann, Bishop Museum)

Elks Club
Macfarlane Home
C. N. Arnold Home and **Park Beach Hotel**
 Castle Estate/Kainalu

The earliest building on this spot was the home of Colonel George W. Macfarlane. The house was later leased to C. N. Arnold, who in 1888 converted it into the *Park Beach Hotel*, considered to be the first beachside hotel.

In 1890, part of Macfarlane's property was sold to the Castle family headed by Samuel N. Castle. Castle came to Hawai'i as a missionary in 1837. In 1851 he and Amos Starr Cooke founded the Castle & Cooke Corporation. His son, James Bicknell Castle, built a huge home here in 1899 and called it *Kainalu* 'billowy sea,' which was said to be the most grandiose home in the islands. *Kainalu* was designed by Oliver G. Traphagen, the same architect who would later design the Moana Hotel (**IX-13**). The Castle home displayed magnificent features: Tiffany stained-glass windows, a *lānai* on each of the levels, and a roof garden with a 360-degree view. The mansion, which was razed in 1959, was so large that it was easily visible a mile offshore.

In 1920 the Elks acquired the building and property and established their club here. Although the original building was completely replaced, its old pilings and foundation can sometimes be seen in the water in front of the club at low tide. The waters one mile offshore, known as Castle's, make for great surfing.

 Kalehuawehe

Hawaiians, especially the royalty, traditionally enjoyed the fine surf of Waikīkī. Though its exact location is no longer known, one of their favorite surfing areas was named *Kalehuawehe*, 'the removed or untied *lei lehua.*' *Kalehuawehe* may have been in the general area of Castle's or as far away as the Moana Hotel, *'Ewa* of here (**III-10**).

There are two Hawaiian legends associated with the name *Kalehuawehe*. According to one legend, the name originated when a young chief from Mānoa (**I-3**) removed his *lei lehua* and gave it to the daughter of Chief Kākuhihewa. Until then, only the princess had been permitted to surf there, but the *kapu*, or taboo, was broken by her accepting the *lei*. The other legend tells of a Hawaiian

✢ 95 ✢

"Robin Hood," Pīkoi, the rat killer, who went to Waikīkī wearing a *lei lehua*. He asked a surfing princess if he could borrow her surfboard, which, of course, she refused because the board was *kapu*. The legend does a flip-flop, however, and they surfed anyway after Pīkoi gave the princess his *lei*!

Continue walking Diamond Head along Kalākaua Avenue.

 Dillingham Fountain

Dillingham Fountain

This graceful fountain was dedicated to Louise Gaylord Dillingham, wife of enterprising Honolulu businessman Walter Dillingham (**VIII-14**), according to the plaque, in appreciation of her services as a member of the Board of Parks and Recreation.

This fountain's predecessor was the *Phoenix Fountain*, erected by the Japanese of Hawai'i in 1919 to represent the joining together of East and West. However, due to anti-Japanese sentiments during World War II, it was razed on December 14, 1942.

Depending on the direction of the wind and where you are standing, you might get a nice cooling-off spray!

In the grassy area Diamond Head of the fountain, take a moment to notice two interesting "only in Hawai'i" items:
• A lava tower built to support the huge, leaning monkeypod tree.
• Hibiscus bushes camouflaging the fountain's mechanical pump.

The pine-like ironwood trees lining Kalākaua Avenue were planted by Archibald Cleghorn (**V-7**) in 1890. Cleghorn was the first commissioner of parks, a governor of Hawai'i, and the husband of Princess Likelike. Near the Diamond Head end of this street are several shower trees with both pink and white blooms. The rainbow shower tree is Honolulu's official tree.

Turn Diamond Head-*mauka* along Poni Mō'ī Street. On the right you will pass Kiele 'gardenia' Avenue.

 Poni Mō'ī Street

Poni Mō'ī has two meanings, depending on whether it is written as one word or two. *Poni Mō'ī*, literally 'royal annointing,' was translated as *coronation*. However, that word was confused with *carnation*, and now *ponimō'ī*, written as one word, refers to the flower. Although the carnation is not native to Hawai'i, it is very popular, grows well here, and is frequently used in *lei*.

Turn away from the beach onto Diamond Head Road, stopping to contemplate the magnificence of Diamond Head. Continue along Diamond Head Road, crossing Coconut Avenue, until you come to Mākālei Place and Mākālei Beach Park (**VIII-13**).

 Diamond Head

Stand at the *'Ewa-mauka* corner of Diamond Head Road and Mākālei Place to gaze up at mighty Diamond Head.

This walk does not take you inside Diamond Head Crater, which last erupted three hundred thousand years ago. However, it will afford a good, close-up view. The entrance to Diamond Head is on the opposite side and is best reached by car. You can walk around inside the crater and walk up to the top of Diamond Head for a spectacular view of Waikīkī.

The name Diamond Head dates from the eighteenth century and refers to the glistening calcite crystals found in the crater by early sailors who mistook the crystals for diamonds.

The crater has also been called Diamond Hill and Kaimana Hill (as in the New Otani Kaimana Beach Hotel, **VIII-6**). Its Hawaiian name is Lēʻahi (a variant of *laeʻahi*), 'forehead of the yellowfin tuna,' because of its profile resembling the brow of forehead of the ʻahi (tuna) fish. But some people, ignoring the long vowel and glottal stop, have suggested a meaning of 'wreath of fire' (*lei ahi*), referring to its history of volcanic activity.

The name Lēʻahi survives as the name of a street on the other side of Diamond Head and as the name of a hospital in Kaimukī (**I-3**).

The crater's highest point, Lēʻahi Peak, is approximately 760 feet (233 meters) above sea level. The most common vegetation inside the gate is non-native; however, there is one special endemic plant, *Bidens cuneata*, which is a composite-type flower related to the daisy and the sunflower. This plant is found only in Hawaiʻi.

On the floor of Diamond Head Crater were structures housing various government operations. Several buildings, including concrete bunkers completed in 1919, are still standing.

The Diamond Head Lighthouse, located further up Diamond Head Road, has been in continuous use since 1899.

 Mākālei Beach Park and Mākālei Place

Mākālei, 'fish trap,' may have been the name of a fishing temple (*heiau*) located on the slopes of Diamond Head.

At the Diamond Head-*mauka* corner of Mākālei Place and Diamond Head Road, take a few minutes to look down at the light green ground cover at your feet: the little yellow-orange flower is the *ʻilima*, native to Hawaiʻi and the official flower of Oʻahu. A one-strand *lei* made from this flower, highly prized, requires seven hundred blossoms!

ʻIlima—the official flower of Oʻahu

Cross Diamond Head Road—carefully! If you have time, stroll over to Mākālei Beach, a pocket beach park. Enjoy the peace and quiet, away from the hustle and bustle of most Waikīkī beaches.

As you return toward Waikīkī along Diamond Head Road, turn Diamond Head on Coconut Avenue, then again walk toward Waikīkī on

WALK VIII ❖ FOOT OF DIAMOND HEAD

Hibiscus. Then walk Diamond Head on Poni Mōʻī up to La Pietra Circle to the grounds of La Pietra Hawaiʻi School for Girls.

14 La Pietra Hawaiʻi School for Girls
Heiau Papaʻenaʻena

La Pietra Hawaiʻi School (Hawaiʻi State Archives)

Since La Pietra is private property, you may prefer to look in quickly and continue reading outside the grounds.

La Pietra, Italian for 'the rock' or 'the gem,' is the name of the residence built here in the 1930s by Walter Dillingham (Dillingham Fountain **VIII-10**). The mansion was built in Mediterranean Revival style, combining characteristics of the original villa in Florence, Italy, where the Dillinghams had been married in 1921, with various innovations of Chicago architect David Adler. Construction is of locally quarried bluestone lava, pink stucco, and red roof tiles.

Unlike other mansions of the time in Waikīkī, this one has survived, now housing La Pietra Hawaiʻi School for Girls. What a lovely setting for a school!

Until 1856 there was a sacrificial *heiau*, 'place of worship,' on the lower level of this site known as *Heiau Papaʻenaʻena*. *Papaʻenaʻena* was probably built later than any other Waikīkī *heiau*, and more is known of this *heiau* than of the others in Waikīkī. *Papaʻenaʻena* means 'forbidding, glowing, red-hot.'

Kahekili, chief of Maui, may have built *Heiau Papaʻenaʻena* in the late 1780s to commemorate his victory over Kahahana, king of Oʻahu, thereby avenging the sacrifice of Kahekili's ancestor Kaʻuhiʻakama at *Heiau ʻĀpuakēhau* (**III-4**).

There are at least six descriptions of this *heiau* as it existed before its final demolition, and each account differs. But all agree that *Heiau Papaʻenaʻena* was extremely large, measuring perhaps 130 feet by 75 feet; its lava wall was 6 to 8 feet tall, ranging from 8 feet thick at its base to 4 feet thick at the top. The side facing the sea would have been open.

Several other well-known Hawaiians were sacrificed here. Among them was Kanihonui, a nephew of Kamehameha I, who had been caught in a compromising situation with Kamehameha I's favorite wife, Kaʻahumanu. Also sacrificed here was Kiana, king of Oʻahu, who had been defeated in the infamous battle of Nuʻuanu in 1795 by Kamehameha I. Kiana's skull, along with skulls of the other defeated warriors, was impaled atop the walls of this *heiau*.

You can return to Diamond Head Road and continue with another walk, either **Walk IX**, Beach Walk, in reverse direction or **Walk VII**, Kapiʻolani Park and the Honolulu Zoo.

❖ 98 ❖

Walk IX
· Beach Walk ·

Walk IX
Beach Walk
Waikīkī Beach from Duke Kahanamoku
Beach and Lagoon to Kapi'olani Park Beach Center

🕐 **TIME:** 1.5 hours

➡ **DISTANCE:** 1.5 miles (2.4 kilometers), mainly in the sand

Kapahulu Pier (IX-19)

THIS IS A LEISURELY WALK ALONG THE LENGTH OF THE SANDS OF WAIKĪKĪ BEACH—PERHAPS THE MOST FAMOUS STRETCH OF BEACH IN THE WORLD! The middle portion overlaps that of **Walk III**, Early Royalty. It is suggested that you read **Walk III** when you arrive at stop **IX-9**, Royal Hawaiian Hotel. The hotels along the beach from the Royal Hawaiian to the Moana are on a site once sacred to Hawaiian chiefs and kings. ❀

▶BEGIN WALK: *This tour starts on the* makai *side of the Hilton Hawaiian Village at the Duke Kahanamoku Beach and Lagoon, and continues along the beach. It stops at most major hotels along the way and ends at Kapi'olani Park Beach Center, near the foot of Diamond Head.*

Take off your shoes and enjoy the walk in the sand!

You can easily take this walk in reverse order, starting from the other end of the beach, at Kapi'olani Park Beach Center.

 1 Duke Kahanamoku Beach and Lagoon/Hilton Lagoon

This beach area and lagoon are named for Hawai'i's best-known sportsman, native-born Hawaiian Duke Paoa Kahanamoku, affectionately known as "the Duke," who won Olympic medals for swimming. In 1912 he won a gold for 100-meter freestyle and a silver for free relay; in 1920, two golds, one in freestyle and one in free relay; and in 1924, a silver in free relay. In 1966 he was the first person to be inducted into the Surfing Hall of Fame. The International Surfing Championship continues to be held in his honor and memory.

The Duke and his eight brothers were raised near here on his mother's family property. He was named for his father, who in turn had been named by Princess Pauahi Bishop in commemoration of the 1869 visit to Hawai'i of Alfred Ernest Albert, Duke of Edinburgh. Paoa, his mother's family name, means 'fragrant.' Kahanamoku translates as 'island work.'

Duke was not only a world-renowned swimmer, but also a movie actor, sheriff of Honolulu, and a true

Kapahulu Pier

WALK IX ✦ BEACH WALK

hero: in 1925 he saved eight people with his surfboard when their boat capsized in the Pacific Ocean off California.

Duke Kahanamoku statue (IX-17)

Duke Kahanamoku Park, just past the Hilton Hawaiian Village, is also named in his memory. At the end of this walk you will encounter his larger-than-life statue (**IX-17**). On August 24, 2002, the 112th anniversary of his birth, the U.S. Postal Service unveiled a stamp to commemorate his life. He died on January 22, 1968.

The Hilton Hawaiian Village sits on most of the property the Paoa family once owned. The land was deeded to Duke's ancestors during the *Mahele* of 1848, the division of Hawaiian land among the rulers and commoners. A Waikīkī Historic Trail marker at the foot of Paoa Road discusses the Duke's mother's family.

Notice all the *hau* trees on the *mauka* side of the lagoon. *Hau* belongs to the Malvaeceae (mallow) family, which includes the hibiscus. In the course of its life (one day!), the *hau* blossom displays three different colors: yellow upon opening, then bright orange, and finally red-brown when it drops. The *hau* tree had many traditional uses: its rough but lightweight wood was used for making canoe outriggers; its fibers were made into rope; and its sap and flowers were used medicinally.

Walk along the beach toward Diamond Head.

Hilton Hawaiian Village
Niumalu Hotel
Hawai'i Kai Beach Club Hotel
2

In the early 1890s, the first commercial structure on this beach was a bathhouse–boarding house called *Ola Waikīkī*. By the early 1900s, it had become more of a boarding house, first under the ownership of John and Eliza Cassidy, who called their hotel *Cassidy's-at-the-Beach*, and later as the *Pierpont Hotel*. Several bathhouses and boarding houses in Waikīkī were first established as annexes of the downtown Honolulu hotels. In 1922, under J. F. Child, this

Hilton Hawaiian Village (1950s–90s)

building was used as an annex for his downtown hotel. However, in the mid-1920s, the property and several other boarding houses in the immediate area were bought up by Afong Heen, a local Chinese merchant

Walk IX
Beach Walk

- **IX-1** Duke Kahanamoku Beach and Lagoon/Hilton Lagoon
- **IX-2** Hilton Hawaiian Village
  - *Niumalu Hotel*
  - *Hawai'i Kai Beach Club Hotel*
- **IX-3** Fort DeRussy Beach
  - *Saratoga Bath House*
- **IX-4** *Kawehewehe*
- **IX-5** Halekūlani Hotel
  - *House Without a Key*
- **IX-6** Gray's Beach
  - *Gray's-by-the-Sea*
- **IX-7** Sheraton Waikīkī Hotel
  - *Wilder Home*
  - *Waikīkī Villa Bath House*
- **IX-8** *Kahaloa*
- **IX-9** Sheraton Royal Hawaiian Hotel
  - *Seaside Hotel*
  - *Helumoa*
- **IX-10** Outrigger Waikīkī Hotel
  - *Outrigger Canoe Club*
- **IX-11** *'Āpuakēhau Stream*
- **IX-12** *Kalehuawehe*
- **IX-13** Sheraton Moana Surfrider Hotel
  - *Moana Hotel*
  - *SurfRider Hotel*
  - *Long Branch Bath House*
  - *Ulukou*
- **IX-14** Waikīkī Beach Center
  - *Police Station*
  - *Waikīkī Bowling Alley*
  - *Waikīkī Inn and Tavern*
  - *Pualeilani*
  - *Kapuni*
- **IX-15** Kāhuna Stones
- **IX-16** Kūhiō Beach Park
  - *Hamohamo*
  - *Uluniu*
- **IX-17** Duke Kahanamoku Statue
- **IX-18** *Kuekaunahi Stream*
- **IX-19** Kapahulu Pier/Queen's Promenade
  - *The Wall*
  - *Kapahulu Avenue*
- **IX-20** Queen's Surf Beach
  - *Deering-Holmes Estate*
  - *Heiau Kupalaha*
- **IX-21** Kapi'olani Park Beach Center
  - *Publics*

and architect. Heen renovated and enlarged these structures, and turned them into the first large hotel on this site: the *Niumalu Hotel*. The name lives on as the Niumalu Restaurant in the Hilton's Kālia Tower. In 1951 the building was replaced by Henry Kaiser's *Hawai'i Kai Beach Club*. In 1956 Conrad Hilton purchased the property, and the *Beach Club* was incorporated into the then-new Hilton Hawaiian Village.

The first color television shows in Hawai'i were seen at the Hilton on May 5, 1957, at *the Dome* (**II-12**).

The newest Hilton building is the Kālia Tower, on the 'Ewa portion of the Village property.

If you would like to come off the beach and walk around the grounds of the Hilton Hawaiian Village, please refer to **Walk II**, stops **10** through **14**.

Notice the stately palm trees on the beach. If you find some shade, remember that it "moves around," following the sun! Unfortunately, many of the trees have recently succumbed to the chopping block. Most likely, these trees are descendants of the trees during the time of the Hawaiian monarchy.

Fort DeRussy Beach Saratoga Bath House

This beach, like all beaches in Hawai'i, is public property although it serves mainly the military and their families staying at the Hale Koa 'house of the warrior' Hotel (**II-3**). The property in this area has been owned by the United States government since 1904, with various buildings being constructed since then. The most recent addition went up in 1995.

The green building behind the terrace is Battery Randolph, once a coastal auxiliary and now the United States Army Museum of Hawai'i (**II-6**).

The terrace along the Diamond Head end of Fort DeRussy Beach is covered with *hau* leaves. There are two other native plants along here: the endemic (found only in Hawai'i) *'ākia* shrub, with small round leaves, and the *'ilima* ground cover, with light green leaves and a nickel-sized yellow-orange flower.

In the late 1880s, one of the first bathhouses in Waikīkī, the *Saratoga Baths*, prospered in this area. The bathhouse was named for Saratoga Springs in upstate New York, a fashionable hot springs resort at that time.

The Waikīkī Historic Trail marker discusses the life of Chun Afong, the first Chinese millionaire in Hawai'i. His story is covered in **Walk II**.

Kawehewehe (Waikīkī Historic Trail marker)

The beach and waters fronting today's Halekūlani were called *Kawehewehe*, 'the removal,' by the ancient Hawaiians. According to legend, sick and injured people were brought here for curative bathing treatments. Often, a seaweed *lei* was worn, to be removed and left behind as a symbolic request that one's sins, believed to be the cause of illness, be forgiven. Modern-day Hawaiians continue to use the ocean waters therapeutically.

Kawehewehe can also mean 'the opening in the reef,' referring to the reef entrance, offshore channel, and tidal pool in this area.

Continue along the beach by walking along the oceanfront walkway. Look down to see the old steps that used to lead beach walkers through the water's edge.

Halekūlani Hotel
House Without a Key

House Without a Key with a view of the ocean

Notice all the beautiful *naupaka*, or half flower, along the beach. Look closely for its small white flower—you will actually see a half flower. There are many legends concerning this half blossom. One legend involves a maiden who became suspicious of her lover's faithfulness. As a test, she tore the flower in two and gave him one half, asking him to bring back a complete flower as proof of his love. Her lover was unsuccessful.

Another legend involves a related mountain plant that bears an identical flower but has radically different leaves. In this legend, a Hawaiian *Romeo and Juliet*, lovers who had been forbidden to marry because of their different backgrounds and social classes decided to die together. The Hawaiian gods turned the woman into the *naupaka kahakai* (by the sea) and the man into the *naupaka kuahiwi* (mountain), joining their love in spirit.

The Halekūlani's thirty-nine bungalows were demolished in June 1981, leaving only the 1931 former lobby building and the restaurant name, "House Without a Key." That original building now houses the award-winning La Mer and Orchid restaurants.

In the late 1800s Robert Lewers, whose name survives in Lewers Street (**I-16**), built a two-story house for his family on this site. Fishermen who then kept their outrigger canoes under the *hau* trees surrounding the property felt so comfortable and welcomed here that they called the house Halekūlani, 'House Befitting Heaven.'

In 1917 Edward P. Irwin leased the Lewers house and converted it into the *Hau Tree Hotel*. Business was poor, though, and the hotel did not prosper.

Restaurant interior

Clifford and Julia Kimball, who had managed the Hale'iwa Hotel on O'ahu's North Shore, leased the property in 1917 and restored its lovely name, Halekūlani. The Kimballs razed the old Lewers home, and in 1932, with local architect Charles W. Dickey, built the present lobby structure with its eucalyptus wood floors and *koa* furniture. The distinctive roof of the Halekūlani, an elevated, pitched hip roof designed to take advantage of Waikīkī's cool trade winds, is known as the Dickey Roof, which became quite popular. Even the local Neiman Marcus store has incorporated it into its architecture. Kimball also increased the Halekūlani land by acquiring the Gray residence (next stop), Diamond Head of the former Lewers home.

Clifford Kimball died in 1949. Julia Kimball, who was known for the jigsaw puzzles she designed and had cut out by hotel employees, died in 1962. Following her death, the Halekūlani and its five acres were sold for $4.3 million to Norton Clapp, an entrepreneur from the Pacific Northwest. The investment was unsuccessful, and in 1981, the hotel was bought by Mitsui Real Estate Development Company. Three years later, following a complete renovation, the present-day jewel emerged. The famous main building has been saved and is now blended into a beautiful 456-room, oceanfront luxury complex.

In 1925, Earl Derr Biggers published a mystery novel entitled *The House Without a Key*, which took place in a house on the Halekūlani property. Actually, both the house and its address, 3927 Kālia Road (**II-1**), were purely fictitious. However, the *kiawe* tree outside the murdered sea captain's home still stands; the hardwood of the *kiawe* makes excellent charcoal. The Halekūlani responded to this well-known book by naming its bar, and now restaurant, the "House Without a Key." Also mentioned in the novel are offshore floats or rafts. Although they are no longer there, those rafts did exist at the time.

The Chinese detective in Biggers's novel, Charlie Chan, was modeled after Chang Apana, a Honolulu police detective. Chang Apana was born on the Big Island of Hawai'i. He worked there as a cowboy before he moved to Honolulu, bringing with him his notorious whip, which he used while on his police beat.

Be sure to catch a glimpse of the beautiful pool with a mosaic of an orchid, the Halekūlani's logo, on its floor.

Restaurant (Diamond Head in background)

The Halekūlani "beach" is a wooden enclosure Diamond Head of the hotel. The ocean water flows under and around it, ensuring that there is still some sand for the Halekūlani guests. Perhaps you'd like to take a dip in the ocean and rest under the beautiful *hau* tree along this stretch of the beach. This *hau* tree provides much-needed shade. And be sure to come back at night to enjoy the Hawaiian music and dancing under the *kiawe* tree at the "House Without a Key."

 Gray's Beach
Gray's-by-the-Sea

In the late 1880s, Cordelia Brown built a house near the Halekūlani and called it *Oneonta*, an Iroquois name meaning 'place of peace.' Oneonta is also the name of a city in upstate New York, as well as the name of a famous racehorse of the day.

Mrs. Brown's daughter and son-in-law, Mr. and Mrs. J. A. Gillman, built a two-story home on this site in 1903. In 1912 they rented the house to LaVancha M. Gray who turned it into a boarding house, calling it *Gray's-by-the-Sea*, hence the current beach name, Gray's Beach. In 1929 the house and land were sold to Clifford Kimball and incorporated into the Halekūlani.

Gray's Beach has several well-known surfing breaks on the reefs just offshore: Paradise, Number Threes, and Number Fours.

Plumeria flowers

Continue along the ocean walkway in front of the Sheraton Waikīkī Hotel, where you can admire the multitude of plants: *hau*, hibiscus, *naupaka* with its half flower, and plumeria trees.

Sheraton Waikīkī Hotel
Wilder Home
 Waikīkī Villa Bath House

The first nonroyal structure here was the *Waikīkī Villa Bath House*, opened in 1889 as an annex to a Honolulu hotel.

The land occupied by the Sheraton Waikīkī Hotel was a gift from Kīna'u, half sister of Kamehameha III and mother of Kamehameha IV and V, to her namesake Elizabeth Kīna'u Wilder. For many years the Wilder family home was on this site. Then at 4:00 P.M. on February 26, 1969, the family home was razed, and in June 1971, the thirty-one-story Sheraton Waikīkī Hotel opened. In the 1970s all the hotels owned by Sheraton were purchased by Japanese entrepreneur Kenji Osano, under the corporate name of Kyo-Ya Company.

Ride the exterior (*mauka* side) glass elevator to the Hanohano Room for breathtaking views of Waikīkī and the Wai'anae mountain range. *Hanohano* means 'glorious,' as in "what a glorious view!"

Continue walking toward Diamond Head. The next five stops overlap with **Walk III**, Early Royalty, which you may enjoy referring to for more detail.

 Kahaloa

In ancient times, the beach between the present-day Halekūlani and Royal Hawaiian hotels was known as *Kahaloa*. *Kahaloa*, meaning 'long place,' was named for one of the four *kāhuna* who came to Hawai'i from Tahiti in ancient times (**IX-15**). A *kahuna* is a master of a craft or vocation. (In more recent times, outsiders have translated the word as 'priest or sorcerer.')

This beach was considered to be a place of spiritual renewal. *Kahaloa* was noted for its fragrant *līpoa* seaweed,

BEACH WALK ✣ **WALK IX**

Waikīkī c. 1916 (Hawai'i State Archives)

one of the three most popular edible seaweeds. (Remember, the covering of the sushi roll, *nori* in Japanese, is seaweed.)

According to legend, a single-toothed shark lived in the waters of *Kahaloa*. But he's long gone, so don't worry!

 Sheraton Royal Hawaiian Hotel
Seaside Hotel
Helumoa

The oldest known name for this beach area fronting the Royal Hawaiian and Outrigger hotels is *Helumoa*, 'chicken scratch,' the etymology of which comes down to us through legends of old: one of a phantom rooster who scratched the sand, rendering it a special place to plant coconut trees, and another that relates the presence of maggots in the graves of a nearby *heiau* (religious temple) (III-1 to 4).

The *Seaside Hotel* (also known as the *Waikīkī Seaside Hotel*, the *Honolulu Seaside Hotel*, and even the *Waikīkī Honolulu Seaside*) was the first hotel here, having been built in 1894. Just as the other bathhouses and boarding houses in Waikīkī were first established as annexes for Honolulu hotels, so too was the *Waikīkī Seaside*. It was used as the Waikīkī annex of the original Royal Hawaiian Hotel in downtown Honolulu, located on the corner of Hotel and Richard streets. That hotel had been built by King Kamehameha V (Lot Kapuāiwa), grandson of Kamehameha the Great, and was first known simply as the Hawaiian Hotel. Later, during the reign of King Kalākaua, it was renamed the Royal Hawaiian Hotel because of the vibrant social life created there by the Merrie Monarch and his court.

Charmain London and Jack London, both authors, stayed at the *Seaside Hotel*. Jack London is the author of "Chun Ah Chun," a short story based on a local Chinese merchant, Chun Afong, as described in **Walk II**. In her 1971 book, *Our Hawaii*, Charmain London describes the *Seaside Hotel*:

> One large frame house of many rooms, half over the water, reached by a winding driveway from the Main Avenue [Kalākaua

WALK IX ✢ BEACH WALK

Avenue] through a grove of lofty coconut palms, under which are stray large cottages belonging to the hotel. In a rambling one-storied building are the kitchen, the bar, an oriental dining room, and a reception hall, also furnished in Chinese carved woods and splendid fittings that belong to the estate. This hall opens into a circular *lanai* [*lānai*, 'porch'] with frescoed ceiling—a round dining and ballroom open half its disk. Beyond the curving steps, on the lawn toward the sea, grow two huge gnarled *hau* trees, each in the center of a round platform where drinks are served.

The new Royal Hawaiian Hotel opened its doors in Waikīkī on February 1, 1927, to twelve hundred black-tie celebrants. The pink hotel, with its Spanish-Baroque-Moorish style (yes, that's its classification!), was designed by architects Warren and Westmore, who also designed New York's Grand Central Station and Washington, D.C.'s Mayflower Hotel. The Royal Hawaiian Hotel was built by Matson Navigation and Territorial Hotel Company, as was the Princess Ka'iulani in 1954. It was set in a huge expanse of tropical gardens, incorporating the coconut grove of the early monarchs (**III-3**). At that time the gardens extended up to Kalākaua Avenue. Part of that garden is still in evidence today. Facilities included tennis courts and a dance floor on the beach terrace. The hotel immediately became known as "the Pink Palace." The importance of its opening was

The Royal Hawaiian Hotel

celebrated in the song "Royal Hawaiian Hotel," by Mary Puala'a Robins.

During World War II, with the beach lined with barbed wire, the Pink Palace housed navy personnel. After the war, extensive renovations and remodeling were completed. In 1969 the sixteen-story Royal Tower was added to the hotel complex. And in 1975 ownership was transferred to Kyo-Ya Company, a Japanese company that also owns several other hotels in Waikīkī, including the Princess Ka'iulani, Sheraton Waikīkī, and the Moana (including the former *SurfRider*). In the 1980s the Royal Hawaiian Hotel was threatened with demolition and replacement with a modern high-rise structure. Now in these times of appreciating our history and historic structures, this is unthinkable! In February 2002, the Royal Hawaiian celebrated its seventy-fifth anniversary.

The grand entrance, with a porte cochère, is on the *'Ewa* side of the building. The plants are surely descendants of those in the original 1927 garden. Objects of Hawaiian interest are on display in the glass cases in the lower lobby. Historical tours are offered Mondays, Wednesdays, and Fridays at 2:00 P.M.

Outrigger Waikīkī Hotel Outrigger Canoe Club

This area is also part of old *Helumoa*. The hotel is built on the former *'Āpuakēhau Stream* (next stop).

In 1908, the Outrigger Canoe Club leased 1.5 acres of beach from the Queen Emma Estate for surfing and canoe paddling. The Queen Emma Estate continues to own the land occupied by the Outrigger, Surfrider, and Moana hotels.

The beneficiary of the Queen Emma Estate is The Queen's Medical Center in downtown Honolulu. Beachfront land further *'Ewa* is owned by the Kamehamaha Schools for Hawaiian and part-Hawaiian children.

The Outrigger Canoe Club, organized by Alexander Hume Ford with 150 male members, was founded to revive the ancient Hawaiian sport of surfing. Within a year, a women's counterpart was formed, the Uluniu Swim Club, named for the King's Coconut Grove (**III-9**). In 1916, the first official lifesaving course in the United States was taught at the Outrigger Canoe Club. The club relocated in 1963 to the foot of Diamond Head (**VIII-7**).

The Outrigger Hotel was built in 1967 by Roy C. Kelley Jr.—architect, builder, and innkeeper. Today it continues to be independently owned by the Kelley family. The lobby contains several items of local interest: an authentic outrigger canoe and a Polynesian star compass table and explanatory material about ancient voyaging and navigational techniques. Duke's Restaurant is located on the second floor, replete with photos of Duke Kahanamoku, for whom the restaurant was named (**IV-15**).

'Āpuakēhau Stream

Until the 1920s, a river from the mountains of O'ahu flowed into this area and out to the ocean. This was the middle one of three rivers that flowed through Waikīkī.

'Āpuakēhau means 'basket of dew.' The name for this stream may derive from the vast quantities of ti, *hau*, and palm plants that lined its banks.

Until it was diverted by the Mānoa-Pālolo Drainage Canal (**I-17**) in the 1920s to create the Ala Wai Canal, *'Āpuakēhau Stream* flowed from the mountains and emptied *'Ewa* of the Moana Hotel. The royalty rinsed their bodies in this cool, freshwater stream after swimming and surfing in the ocean.

Kalehuawehe

Hawaiians, especially the royalty of old, have traditionally enjoyed the fine surf of Waikīkī. Though its exact location is no longer known, one of the favorite surfing areas was named *Kalehuawehe*, 'the removed or untied *lei lehua*.'

Two legends are associated with the name *Kalehuawehe*. One legend says the name originated when a young chief from Mānoa (**I-3**) removed his *lei lehua* and gave it to the daughter of Chief Kākuhihewa. Until then, only the princess had been permitted to surf there, but the *kapu*, or taboo, was broken by her accepting the *lei*. According to another legend, telling of a Hawaiian "Robin Hood," Pīkoi, the rat killer, went to Waikīkī wearing a *lei lehua*. He asked a surfing princess if he could borrow her surfboard, which, of course, she refused as the board was *kapu*. The legend does a flip-flop, however, and they surfed anyway after Pīkoi gave the princess his *lei!*

Kalehuawehe may have been in the general area of the Moana Hotel or as far away as Castle's, at the foot of Diamond Head (**VIII-9**).

Sheraton Moana Surfrider Hotel
Moana Hotel
SurfRider Hotel
Long Branch Bath House
Ulukou

Sheraton Moana Surfrider Hotel

In the times of the early monarchy, this area fronting the ocean was known as *Ulukou*, 'kou tree grove,' which surrounded the royal residence (**III-8**). It was *kapu*, 'taboo,' to commoners. The *kou* tree is found in the Pacific Islands. *Kou* wood is most useful, and is often carved into bowls, cups, and dishes.

The first nonroyal structure on this former sacred land, and perhaps the first hotel-type structure in Waikīkī, was *Dodd's Long Branch Bath House*, built in 1881 and named for Long Branch, New Jersey, a then-fashionable resort, even for presidents. In 1889 a later owner, Jim Sherwood, added not only more rooms, but also a 200-foot-long toboggan, offering a slide into the ocean 100 feet offshore!

The family residence of Walter Chamberlain Peacock, an English businessman, was located here in the 1890s. Mr. Peacock invested $150,000 in the building of the Moana Hotel, ensuring that he had an office on the top, overlooking the mighty Pacific Ocean. When Hawai'i was still an independent republic, a large new hotel in the middle of Waikīkī was proposed. The idea materialized as the present structure, minus the side wings and two upper floors, which were added in 1918. By that time, Hawai'i had been annexed as a U.S. territory. The hotel building was designed by Minnesota architect Oliver G. Traphagen, who also planned the Archives building in downtown Honolulu, the magnificent Castle home at the Diamond Head end of Waikīkī (**VIII-8**), and the fire station in Pālama on O'ahu.

The colonial-style Moana 'ocean' Hotel, lovingly referred to as "the First Lady of Waikīkī," is Waikīkī's oldest surviving hotel. It opened on March 11, 1901, to serve the classy "steamboat set" from the U.S. mainland. This central 1901 building and the two six-story Italian Renaissance wings built in 1918 are referred to as the Banyan Wing.

The original 1901 Moana, an eclectic style of Colonial and Queen Anne, was four stories tall and contained

BEACH WALK ❖ **WALK IX**

Waikīkī with Moana Hotel in the center (Hawai'i State Archives)

seventy-five rooms. The building's interior is of oak and pine, with each floor decorated with a different wood: the first floor with oak; second, mahogany; third floor, maple; fourth floor, *koa*; and fifth, cherry. On the rooftop was the observation tower that housed Walter Peacock's office. The Banyan Wing, the main and central building, is listed on the National Register of Historic Places and boasts the islands' first electric elevator.

The hotel dining room included a dance floor that extended out over the ocean. Alongside the dining room was a 300-foot pier where locals and tourists walked at night.

Banyan tree in the Moana Hotel's Banyan Court

On July 3, 1935, the popular "Hawai'i Calls" radio program was first broadcast from the Banyan Court of the Moana Hotel. Webley Edwards and Harry Owens were the originators

and producers of the show. Audiences for the broadcast in the courtyard often numbered two thousand. For years there was a plaque on the courtyard's almost 100-year-old banyan tree claiming that Robert Louis Stevenson did much of his writing there. However, this tree and Stevenson never met: the tree was planted in 1904, but Stevenson had died in Sāmoa ten years earlier. So much for historical authenticity! This banyan tree, 75 feet tall and 150 feet across, is on Hawai'i's Rare and Exceptional Tree list, giving it protection under state law.

During World War II, while the Royal Hawaiian was leased to the navy and Waikīkī Beach was lined with barbed wire, the Moana Hotel continued to provide its guests with its customary elegance.

The original *SurfRider Hotel* opened in 1952 as Waikīkī's first post-Moana high-rise hotel. Today this eight-story building comprises the Diamond Wing of the Moana Hotel on the Diamond Head side of the Banyan Wing. In 1969 the next *SurfRider Hotel* was built 'Ewa of the Moana Hotel, on a portion of the site of the filled-in streambed of the 'Āpuakēhau Stream. This twenty-one-story building, the Tower Wing, is on the 'Ewa side of the Banyan Wing.

WALK IX ÷ BEACH WALK

In 1987 the hotel's name was officially changed to Sheraton Moana Surfrider Hotel. In 1989, it began a $50 million renovation, which lasted almost two years. The refurbishment returned many aspects of the hotel to its original 1901 architecture, transporting guests back to its Victorian origins. The beautifully restored hotel reopened in March 1989.

Do spend some time in the Moana's Historical Room, which is replete with video footage of old Waikīkī, photos, artifacts, and facts, on the second floor. Historical tours are offered throughout the week; check on dates and times in the main lobby.

Walk Diamond Head through the main lobby and the Moana's Diamond Wing, then exit onto Kalākaua Avenue.

Waikīkī Beach Center
Police Station
Waikīkī Bowling Alley
Waikīkī Inn and Tavern
Pualeilani
 ### *Kapuni*

Waikīkī Beach Center, the area between the Moana complex and Kūhiō Beach, is land once owned by King Kamehameha IV, who deeded it to a missionary physician. Prince Kūhiō's home, *Pualeilani*, was located approximately where today's surfboard stand is situated, *makai* of the police station.

In the late 1890s, bathhouses similar to the *Long Branch* also existed along here: *Ilaniwai Baths* and *Wright's Villa*. By 1900, the property was turned into the Waikīkī Inn and Tavern.

In the first three-quarters of the twentieth century, this area was a popular place, with stores, inns, taverns, restaurants, and even a bowling alley. With the building of the *SurfRider Hotel*, now the Diamond Wing of the Moana Hotel, in 1950–52, all that changed. Before the *SurfRider* went up, there was a string of homes and small, but very popular, businesses, some of which remained until the 1970s. These included the *Waikīkī Tavern*, built in 1884, later known as the *Waikīkī Inn and Tavern*, with the *Waikīkī Surf Club* housed in the lower level; the all-you-can-eat buffet for seventy-five cents at the *Waikīkī Sands Restaurant*; the *Merry-Go-Round Bar*; the *Huddles Restaurant*; *Heine's*, a popular drinking establishment (until Prohibition!); and *Waikīkī Bowling*. Some of the nonroyal homes along here were the residences of the Cunhas, the Steiners, and the Hustaces.

Waikīkī Inn and Tavern, *1945 (Ray Jerome Bakee, Bishop Museum)*

In earlier times, the surfing area offshore was named *Kapuni*, meaning 'the surrounding,' after a *kahuna* who came from a faraway land. This area was the *kahuna*'s favorite surfing spot. Kapuni Street is located between Kūhiō Avenue and Cleghorn Street (**Walk V**).

BEACH WALK ✦ **WALK IX**

Today, the surfing areas offshore are known as Taverns and Cunha's. Continue along to the fenced-in boulders.

 Kāhuna Stones

Kāhuna Stones

Bird's eye view of the Kāhuna Stones

The gems of Waikīkī! These stones are located on the sand near the Waikīkī Beach Center pavilion and are surrounded by native *naupaka* plants (**IX-5**). The four Kāhuna Stones, also referred to as the Wizard Stones and the Healing Stones, are the most sacred vestige of old Waikīkī. Please afford them the respect they deserve.

These revered stones have recently been enclosed and have been joined, in commemoration, by a similar fifth stone from Tahiti. The beautiful renovation was done by Billy Fields, from the Big Island of Hawai'i. Notice that the lava stones at the base of the iron fence are not held together by mortar. This ancient Hawaiian method of stone setting is called dry-stack rock construction. The rocks are carefully placed so they fit and "lock" into place.

The stones commemorate four legendary *kāhuna*, Hawaiian master craftsmen or professionals. They were known as Kapaemahū, Kinohi, Kapuni, and Kahaloa. After arriving from Tahiti, most likely in the fourteenth century, they settled in *Ulukou* (**IX-13**), where they exercised their enormous healing powers. Hawaiians came from afar to be cured. When the *kāhuna* left Hawai'i, four large commemorative boulders were brought in from Kaimukī (**I-3**). The stones were originally set in different locations. Kapuni's stone was placed where the surf meets the beach, lending his name to an ancient surfing area. The stones of Kapaemahū and Kinohi were set above the shoreline at *Ulukou*, where the *kāhuna* lived. And the stone of Kahaloa was placed on the 'Ewa bank of '*Āpuakēhau Stream*, lending his name to the beach. After a ceremony transferring their power to those rocks, the four *kāhuna* departed.

Over time, these sacred stones were scattered around Waikīkī, only to be rediscovered at various places, including at '*Āinahau* and under the former *Waikīkī Bowling Alley*!

The plaque reads:

> In 1997, the stones were raised onto a *paepae* (stone platform), and an *ahu* (altar) and fence were built to honor and protect them. The largest stone was estimated to weigh

WALK IX ÷ BEACH WALK

7.5 tons. As part of the project ceremonies, Tahitians from Raiatea presented a stone from the healers' homeland, which they named *Ta'ahu Ea* (the life).

These ancient stones are part of the spiritual history of Waikīkī and the native Hawaiian people. They remind us of the need to preserve and honor Hawai'i's unique heritage for generations to come.

Kāhuna Stones plaque

If this interests you, be sure to read *The Kāhuna: Versatile Masters of Old Hawai'i*, by Likeke R. McBride, lovingly edited by his son, Andrew S. McBride.

 Kūhiō Beach Park
Hamohamo
Uluniu

Kūhiō Beach stretches from Waikīkī Beach Center to the grassy area on the beach.

Kūhiō Beach Park is named for Prince Jonah Kūhiō Kalaniana'ole, whose home, *Pualeilani*, was nearby. When Kūhiō's mother died shortly after his birth in 1871, he and his brothers (**V-2** to **4**) were adopted by their aunt, Kalākaua's wife. When Kalākaua became king in 1874, he gave royal titles to his sisters, Lili'uokalani (**V-10**) and Miriam Likelike (**V-9**), and to his foster child, Kūhiō.

Queen Lili'uokalani, who owned this area, known as *Hamohamo*, 'rub gently,' referring to the ocean lapping at the shore, later gave a portion of her estate to Kūhiō. *Hamohamo*, bordered by *'Āpuakēhau Stream* on the *'Ewa* side and *Kuekaunahi Stream* on the Diamond Head side, extended back past present-day Ala Wai Canal.

Since King Kalākaua and Queen Kapi'olani owned a summer home here, it was probably they who gave the property its name, *Pualeilani*, meaning 'flower from the wreath of heaven' or 'the royal perfume.' *Pualeilani* was also used by Queen Lili'uokalani as the name of one of her homes.

Uluniu, 'coconut grove,' referred to a grove of several thousand coconut trees that surrounded King Kalākaua's residence here. Many of the coconut trees in Waikīkī today are descendants of trees from the time of the early Hawaiians.

Uluniu Avenue is *mauka*-Diamond Head, and is named in honor of the royalty who once lived here.

Prince Kūhiō served as a delegate

Diamond Head from Waikīkī Beach, Kūhiō Beach site c. 1935 (Hawai'i State Archives)

BEACH WALK ✦ **WALK IX**

Waikīkī coconut grove, c. 1890 (Hawai'i State Archives)

to the United States Congress from 1902 until his death in 1922 at the age of fifty. He was instrumental in enacting the 1920 Hawaiian Homes Commission Act, which granted two hundred thousand acres of land to Native Hawaiians. Kūhiō's death marked the end of an era: the royal realm at Waikīkī would be no longer. This beach was dedicated to him in 1940. Prince Kūhiō was fondly referred to by many nicknames, including Prince Cupid, the Chief of the People, and the Citizen's Prince. Prince Kūhiō Day, an official state holiday, is celebrated on March 26.

Walk up to the street to the statue of Duke Kahanamoku.

 Duke Kahanamoku Statue

Duke Kahanamoku appears larger than life in this beautifully crafted bronze statue. Full-blooded Hawaiian, born and raised in Waikīkī, he was well loved in Hawai'i, not only for winning Olympic silver and gold medals in swimming, but also as a hero, movie actor, and Honolulu sheriff (**IX-1**). A surfboard is strategically placed behind him. Ironically, his back is to the ocean, which has generated some controversy, since it is contrary to Hawaiian custom.

Local lore has it that the Duke rode the longest wave ever: a mile and a quarter on a thirty-five-foot wave!

 Kuekaunahi Stream

Kuekaunahi Stream originally flowed down from the mountains, through Pālolo Valley (**I-3**) and into Waikīkī. It emptied into the ocean 'Ewa of Kapahulu Pier (next stop) and the Wall. However, in the 1920s, *Kuekaunahi Stream* was diverted away

Kapahulu Pier

WALK IX ✦ BEACH WALK

from Waikīkī into the Mānoa-Pālolo Drainage Canal (**I-17**) (not a very picturesque name, is it?!), and out to the Pacific Ocean via the Ala Wai Canal.

Today, the only reminder of *Kuekaunahi Stream* in Waikīkī is a break in the reef offshore.

Kapahulu Pier/Queen's Promenade
The Wall
19 Kapahulu Avenue

Kapahulu Avenue (**VI-8**) forms the Diamond Head boundary of Waikīkī proper; greater Waikīkī extends up to the slope of Diamond Head.

Kapahulu has two very different interpretations in Hawaiian: 'the worn-out soil' and 'a feather garment.' The latter may have referred to a feather garment worn by King Lunalilo, who owned a tract of land in the area.

Extending into the water from the end of Kapahulu Avenue is Kapahulu Pier, recently renamed, more picturesquely, Queen's Promenade. A walk to the gazebo at the end of the pier is absolutely lovely. Do go! Perpendicular to the pier is "slippery wall," obviously so named because it can be dangerously slick. It was originally built to keep the beach from eroding; unfortunately, it has not helped much.

Notice the beautifully appointed lava walls interspersed with pools of water and small waterfalls.

The beach area between the Wall and the Natatorium (**VIII-3**) has recently been established as the protective Waikīkī Marine Life Conservation District. This means nothing may be taken from the beach or the ocean: no sand, no rocks, no coral, no marine animals.

Queen's Surf Beach
Deering-Holmes Estate
20 Heiau Kupalaha

Queen's Surf Beach extends from the Wall to the Waikīkī Aquarium. On some weekend evenings, movies are shown at sunset. This beach is named in honor of Queen Kapi'olani (**VII-1**).

The first nonroyal residence here belonged to the Charles Deering family, and later, in the 1930s, to Christopher Holmes. During World War II, the *Deering-Holmes Estate* served as a conference center for President Roosevelt.

In 1946 the mansion was converted into the *Queen's Surf Restaurant*. Its entertainment area, known as the *Barefoot Bar*, was a popular center of Hawaiian music and dance. Although the City and County of Honolulu obtained the land in 1953, the restaurant was allowed to continue operations. In 1961 the Spencecliff Corporation leased the restaurant for ten years, and the *Queen's Surf* became known for its beach *lū'au*. When the Spencecliff lease expired in 1971, the

Kapahulu Pier from water

mansion-turned-restaurant was demolished to create more open space along the beach.

Heiau Kupalaha was a religious structure located at Queen's Surf Beach. It is thought that it operated in conjunction with *Heiau Papa'ena'ena* (**VIII-14**) on the slope of Diamond Head.

The surfing area here is not called Queens—Queens is located off Waikīkī Beach Center, as is Baby Queens. The surfing area between here and the Wall is known as Cunha's.

Kapi'olani Park Beach Center
Publics

The building housing the public baths, dressing rooms, and refreshment stand is known as the Kapi'olani Park Beach Center, named in memory of Queen Kapi'olani, the wife of King David Kalākaua. The history of public baths at this location reflects the city's attempt to make available to the public all of Waikīkī's beaches. In the 1880s the beaches began to be encumbered by houses built along the shore. Access to the beaches gradually became limited to property owners. In 1908 the City and County of Honolulu obtained the land. A public bath facility was constructed, complete with showers, dressing rooms, lounges, and a dance pavilion, hence the nickname Publics. The surfing area offshore is known as Publics.

One of the earliest structures on this site was the original Aquarium (**VIII-1**), built in 1904.

This is the conclusion of **Walk IX**. If you have not yet taken **Walk VIII**, Foot of Diamond Head, the beginning of the walk is at the Waikīkī Aquarium, just Diamond Head of Kapi'olani Park Beach Center.

FURTHER READING

Beckwith, Martha Warren. *Hawaiian Mythology*. Honolulu: University of Hawai'i Press, 1970.

Budnick, Rich, and Duke Kalani Wise. *Hawaiian Street Names: The Complete Guide to O'ahu Street Name Translations*. Honolulu: Aloha Publishing, 1989.

Cohen, Stan. *The First Lady of Waikīkī: A Pictorial History of the Sheraton Moana Surfrider*. Missoula, Montana: Pictorial Histories Publishing Company, Inc., 2000.

Cohen, Stan. *The Pink Palace: The Royal Hawaiian Hotel, A Sheraton Hotel in Hawaii*. Missoula, Montana: Pictorial Histories Publishing Company, Inc., 1986.

Cohen, Stan. *Princess Kaiulani and the Princess Kaiulani Hotel in Waikīkī*. Missoula, Montana: Pictorial Histories Publishing Company, Inc., 1997.

'Ī'ī, John Papa. *Fragments of Hawaiian History*. Honolulu: Bishop Museum Press, 1973.

Kamakau, Samuel M. *Ka Poe Kahiko: The People of Old*. Honolulu: Bernice P. Bishop Museum, Special Publication 51, 1964.

Kamakau, Samuel M. *Ruling Chiefs of Hawai'i*. Honolulu: The Kamehameha Schools, 1961.

Kanahele, George S. *Waikīkī: 100 B.C. to 1900 A.D., An Untold Story*. Honolulu: The Queen Emma Foundation, 1995.

Lili'uokalani. *Hawaii's Story by Hawaii's Queen*. Tokyo: Charles E. Tuttle Co., Inc., 1979.

London, Charmain. *Our Hawaii*. New York: MacMillan Co., 1922.

McAllister, J. Gilbert. *The Archeology of O'ahu*. Honolulu: Bernice P. Bishop Museum, Publication 104, 1972. Reprint of 1933 edition.

McBride, Likeke R. *The Kāhuna: Versatile Masters of Old Hawai'i*. Hilo: Petroglyph Press Ltd., 2000.

Pukui, Mary Kawena, and Samuel H. Elbert. *Hawaiian Dictionary*. Honolulu: University of Hawai'i Press, 1971.

Pukui, Mary Kawena, Samuel H. Elbert, and Esther T. Mookini. *Place Names of Hawai'i*. Honolulu: University of Hawai'i Press, 1974.

Schütz, Albert J. *Things Hawaiian: A Pocket Guide to the Hawaiian Language*. Honolulu: Island Heritage, 1997.

Seiden, Allan. *Waikīkī: Magic Beside the Sea*. Hong Kong: Island Heritage, 2001.

INDEX

To show how longer Hawaiian words are pronounced, accent units (see the Guide to Pronunciation) are separated by periods. A * before a word indicates that we do not know its proper pronunciation with respect to long vowels, glottal stops, and accent. Historic sites, no longer in existence, are in italics. The names of the walks appear in capitals.

Afong, Chun — 20, 107
'Āina.hau — 8, 56
'Āina.hau Park — 59
'Āina.kea Way — 5, 71
Ala Moana Hotel — 51
Ala Moana Shopping Center — 51
ALA WAI CANAL — 1, 2, 4
Ala Wai Golf Course and Club — 4
Ala Wai Marina and Boat Harbor — 28
Ala Wai Playing Field and Park — 9
Ala Wai Promenade — 13
Aloha Amusement Park — 28
Apana, Chang — 105
'Ā.pua.kē.hau Heiau — 8, 34, 36
'Ā.pua.kē.hau Stream 8, 9, 36, 47, 109, 111
Archery range — 76
'Au.'au.kai — 56

Banyan tree — 48, 56, 60, 111
Battery Randolph — 20
BEACH WALK — 99
Biggers, Earl Derr — 105
Bishop Museum — 26, 36
Bishop, Princess Pau.ahi — 23, 26
Brothers in Valor Memorial Park — 43
Brown, Francis 'Ī'ī — 4
Buckminster Fuller Dome — v, 25

Cartwright, Alexander Joy Jr. — 20, 70
Cartwright Road — 70
Castle Estate/Kainalu — 95
Castle's surfing area — 95
Charlot, Jean — 50
Charlot, Jean, fresco murals — 50
Chinese duck and rice fields 2, 11, 16, 28
Chinese in Wai.kī.kī — 2, 11, 16, 20, 29

"Chun Ah Chun" — 20, 107
Cleghorn Street — 61
Cleghorn, Archibald — 61, 80, 88, 96
C. N. Arnold Home — 95
Coconut Avenue — 11, 96
Community gardens — 75
Cook, Captain — 10
Cunha, Emmanuel — 47, 88

Dailey, Gardner — 46, 58
Damien Museum — 70
Deering-Holmes Estate — 91, 116
Diamond Head — 96
Diamond Head Community
 Gardens — 75
Dickey, Charles W., architect 44, 91, 105
Dillingham Fountain — 96
Dome, the — v, 25
Duke Kahana.moku Beach and
 Lagoon — 27, 100
Duke Kahana.moku Park — 23
Duke Kahana.moku Statue — 115
Duke's Lane — 45
Duke's Restaurant — 45, 49, 109

EARLY HAWAIIAN LIFE IN
 WAI.KĪ.KĪ: KĀLIA — 15
EARLY ROYALTY — 31
Elks Club — 94, 95
Emma, Queen — 46, 109
'Ena Road — 29

Fayerweather, Julia — 20
First Hawaiian Bank — 50
FOOT OF DIAMOND HEAD — 87

Fort DeRussy	20	'Ili.kai	27
Fort DeRussy Beach	22, 103	'Ilima	xv, 97
		International Market Place	46
Gardens of the Hilton Hawaiian			
Village	24	Jefferson Elementary School	71
Gray's Beach	105	Jefferson School Orthopedic Unit	71
Gray's-by-the-Sea	105	Joggers' Rest	82
Green flash	27	Jungle, the	61
Gump Building	43		
Gump's	43	Ka'ahu.manu	xiv, 10, 35, 36, 92, 98
		Kaha.loa	106, 113
Hale Koa Hotel	18	Kahana.moku, Duke	22, 23, 74, 92
Hale.kū.lani Hotel	104	*Kahe.kili	xiii, 36, 37, 98
Hamo.hamo	37, 62, 114	Kāhi Hāli'a Aloha	85
Hau	5, 37, 74	Kahua.moko.moko Athletic Field	36
Hau Tree Beach Bar	24	Kāhuna Stones	113
Hau Tree Hotel	104	Kai.nalu	95
Hau Tree Lānai restaurant	93, 94	Kai.'olu Street	9
Hawai'i Convention Center	12, 13	Kaiser, Henry	24
Hawai'i Kai Beach Club Hotel	24, 102	Ka'iu.lani Avenue	8, 56, 58
Hawaiian Burial Memorial	85	Ka'iu.lani, Princess	xiv, 8, 56, 60
Hawaiian Taro Fields and		*Kā.kuhi.hewa	32, 38, 95
Fishponds	16, 27	Kā.lai.moku Street	10
Heiau 'Ā.pua.kē.hau	8, 34, 36	Kalā.kaua Avenue	12, 40
Heiau Kupa.laha	91, 116	Kalā.kaua, King David	12, 40, 54, 59,
Heiau Papa.'ena.'ena	36, 98	64, 78, 83, 114	
Heine's Tavern	112	Kalani.nui.ahi.lapa.lapa	56
Helu.moa	32, 34, 107	Kale.hua.wehe	38, 95, 109
Helu.moa Road	32	Kā.lia	16
Hilton Hawaiian Village	24, 102	Kā.lia Road	18
Hilton Lagoon	27	Kā.lia Tower	25, 36
Hobart, Louis	91	*Kaluaokau	46
Hobron Lane	28	Kama.kau, Samuel, historian	18
Honolulu Marathon	78	Kameha.meha I	xiv, 10, 32
Honolulu Zoo	57, 85	Kameha.meha II	xiv, 10, 92
Hotel Niu.malu	24, 102	Kameha.meha III	viii, xiv, 18, 35
House Without a Key	104	Kameha.meha IV	xiv, 47, 112
Hustace, Frank	47	Kameha.meha V	xiv, 35, 63, 107
Hyatt Regency Wai.kī.kī Hotel	46	Kāne.kapō.lei Street	9, 60
		Kāne.loa	64, 71, 78
'Ī'ī, John Papa	18	Kāne.loa Road	64, 71
Ikesu Hotel and Café	27	Kani.honui	98
Ilani.wai Baths	112	Kapa.hulu Avenue	72, 116

❈ 120 ❈

Kapa.hulu Pier 115, 116
Kapili Street 62
Kapi'o.lani Bandstand 81
Kapi'o.lani Park 57, 76, 78, 117
KAPI'O.LANI PARK AND
  HONOLULU ZOO 77
Kapi'o.lani Park Beach Center 117
Kapi'o.lani, Queen 70, 74, 78, 81, 116
Kapua 88, 92
Kapua Channel 92
Kapuni 112
Kawehe.wehe 34, 103
Kea.lohi.lani Avenue 63
Ke'eli.kō.lani, Princess Ruth 56
Kekio 64, 71
Keoni.ana Street 11
Kiawe tree 105
Kiele Avenue 96
Kī.na'u 18, 106
King Kalā.kaua Plaza 43
King's Coconut Grove 37
King's Park and Grove 34
King's Village Shopping Center 58
Koa Avenue 59
Koa wood in McDonald's at
  Discovery Bay 28
Kua.mo'o Street 10
**Kuekaunahi Stream* 7, 37, 62, 64, 115
Kū.hiō Avenue 40, 42
Kū.hiō Beach Park 64, 114
Kū.hiō, Prince 38, 59, 64, 112, 114
Kū.ihe.lani 34
Kupa.laha Heiau 91, 116
Kuroda Field 19
Kyo-Ya Company 6, 48

La Pietra Hawai'i School
  for Girls 98
LAST DAYS OF THE
  MONARCHY 53
Lau.niu Street 9
Lemon Road 70
Lewers Street 9, 104

Liberty House 45
Like.like, Princess 56, 61, 62
Lili'u.cka.lani Avenue 9, 62
Lili'u.cka.lani, Queen xiv, 7, 9, 54, 62,
  63, 114
Lī.pe'e.pe'e Street x, 13
LOCAL LIFE TODAY
  IN WAI.KĪ.KĪ 67
London, Charmain 107
London, Jack 107
Long Branch Bath House 110
Luna.lilo, King xiv, 46, 72, 116

Macfa-lane Home 95
Macy's Department Store 45
Mahatma Gandhi Statue 84
Mahele of 1848 viii, 88, 102
Maile xvii, 19
Mā.'i.i.kū.kahi 32
Mā.kā.lei Beach Park/
  Mā.kā.lei Place 97
Makee Island 84
Makee Road 84
Mak.ki 6, 12
Mak.ki Stream 12
Malu.hia Road 19
Mā.noa-Pā.lolo Drainage Canal 9
Mā.noa Valley 6
Matson Navigation 6, 58, 108
McCully Street 11
McDonald's at Discovery Bay 28
McDuff Park 13
McInerny Estate 94
MIRACLE MILE 39
Moana Hotel 47, 110
Mō.'ili.'ili 6
Monsarrat Avenue 75, 78, 85

Nā.hua Street 9
Nā.mā.hana Street 10
Natatorium 91
Nau.paka flower 22, 90
New Otani Kai.mana Beach Hotel 93,
  94, 97

Niu.malu Hotel	*24, 102, 103*	Queen's Surf Beach	91, 116
Niu Street	11		
Noho.nani Street	9	*Racetrack*	*82*
Nu'u.anu	59, 98	Radisson Wai.kī.kī Prince	
		Kū.hiō Hotel	62
Ohana Edgewater Hotel	51	Rainbow mural on the Hilton	
'Ō.hua Avenue	8, 63	Rainbow Tower	26
'Olo.hana Street	10	Rainbows	7
Outrigger Canoe Club	45, 94, 109	Renaissance 'Ili.kai Hotel and	
Outrigger Canoe Club, original		Apartments	27
location	*49*	Ridges and valleys beyond	
Outrigger Wai.kī.kī Hotel	34, 49, 60, 109	Wai.kī.kī	5
		Ripley, Clinton Briggs, architect	56
Pā.kī Avenue	74	Royal Hawaiian Hotel	36, 107
Pā.kī Hale	76	Royal Hawaiian Shopping Center	49
Pā.kī Park	74		
Pā.kī Playground	74	Sans Souci Beach	93
Pā.lolo Valley	6, 115	*Sans Souci Hotel*	*93*
Paoa family	18, 102	*Saratoga Bath House*	*103*
Paoa.kalani Street	8, 63, 71	Saratoga Road	22
Paoa Place	18, 23	Seaside Avenue	9, 44
Papa.'ena.'ena Heiau	*36, 98*	Sheraton Moana Surfrider	
Park Beach Hotel	*95*	Hotel	47, 110
Pa'ū Street	11	Sheraton Princess Ka'iu.lani Hotel	56, 58
Peacock residence	*46*	Sheraton Royal Hawaiian Hotel	36, 107
Peacock, Walter	46, 48, 110	Sheraton Wai.kī.kī Hotel	106
People's open market	66, 75	St. Augustine Church	63, 68, 71
Pi'i.naio Stream	*10, 16, 27*	Steiner, Judge	47, 112
Police Station	47, 112	Stevenson, Robert Louis	42, 48, 56, 60,
Poni Mō.'ī Street	96	61, 93, 111	
Prince Edward Street	59	*SurfRider Hotel*	*47, 110, 112*
Prince Kūhio Hotel	62		
Princess Ka'iu.lani Hotel	56, 58		
Princess Ka'iu.lani Park	59	Tapa	25, 81
Princess Ka'iu.lani Shops	46	Tapa Tower	24, 81
Pua.ali'i.li'i or Pua'a.li'i.li'i	*34*	Taro fields	16, 18, 61, 73
Pua.lani Way	64, 71	Thurston Circle	72
Pua.lei.lani	*47, 65, 112*	Time capsule	81
Publics	117	Ti plant	6, 73
		Traphagen, Oliver G., architect	48, 95, 110
Queen Kapi'o.lani Hibiscus Garden	74	Trolley	13, 40, 82
Queen Kapi'o.lani Statue	81	Trolley stop and shelter	82
Queen's Promenade	116	Tusi.tala Street	61

Ulu.kou   37, 110
Ulu.niu   37, 58, 64, 109, 114
Ulu.niu Avenue   37, 38, 65
University Avenue   10
University of Hawai'i   6, 10, 26, 83, 90
U.S. Army Museum of Hawai'i   20

Vancouver, Captain   viii
Verne, Jules   27

Wai.'anae Mountains   28, 106
Wai.kī.kī Aquarium   82, 90
Wai.kī.kī Beach Center   112
Wai.kī.kī Beach Marriott Hotel   64
Wai.kī.kī Bowling Alley   47, 112
Wai.kī.kī Business Plaza   44
Wai.kī.kī Community Center
       Complex   71
Wai.kī.kī Fire Station: Station No. 7   73
Wai.kī.kī Gateway Park   40
Wai.kī.kī Inn and Tavern   47, 112
Wai.kī.kī-Kapahulu Public Library   72
Wai.kī.kī Park   28
Wai.kī.kī School   75
Wai.kī.kī Seaside Hotel   9, 44, 107
Wai.kī.kī Shell amphitheater   83
Wai.kī.kī Theater   44
Wai.kī.kī Villa Bath House   106
Wai.kī.kī Walk at the Galleria   44
Wai.kī.kī Yacht Club   28
Wai.kolu Way   2
Wai Nani Way   7, 63
Walina Street   9, 60
Wall, the   116
War Memorial Natatorium   91
Wilder Home   106
Wright's Villa   112

Young, John I   10
Young, John II   11

Zoo, Honolulu   57, 85

From the streets of New York City the author came to Hawai'i, where she earned her doctorate in linguistics from the University of Hawai'i and became enamored of the history and culture of the islands. Having lived in various places around the world, including Athens, Greece; Tripoli, Libya; and Paris, France, Dr. Acson found true paradise in Waikīkī, the home of her heart. While living there, she began tracing the origins of the street names and unearthed fascinating remnants and representations of Hawaiian history that remain to this day.

After pursuing studies and employment in language, linguistics, and neurolinguistics, the author moved to the Washington, DC, area, where she currently resides with Howard, Samantha, Nick, and Hank—and dreams about Waikīkī.